THE AI REVOLUTION IS HERE

PREPARING THE WORKFORCE FOR CHANGE

BY CHRISTOPHER K. BOUCHER, ESQ.

A PRACTICAL GUIDE WITH INSIGHTS INTO
LEGAL AND EMPLOYMENT ISSUES INVOLVING
THE ADOPTION OF AI FOR THE WORKFORCE

WWW.AIREVOLUTION.LAW

Jacobs & Whitehall
9600 Escarpment Blvd
Suite 745-282
Austin, TX 78749
(888) 570-7338
www.jacobsandwhitehall.com

Ordering Information:

Quantity sales. Special discounts are available on quantity purchases by corporations, associations, and others. For details, contact the publisher at the address above.

Orders by U.S. trade bookstores and wholesalers. Please contact Jacobs & Whitehall: Tel: (888) 570-7338 or visit www.jacobsandwhitehall.com.

Printed in the United States of America

Published in 2024

ISBN: 978-1-963063-01-1

Dedication

To Gene - Life is all about taking chances. Thank you for always betting on me, time and time again.

Disclaimer

This publication is intended to be used for educational purposes only. No legal advice is being given, and no attorney-client relationship is intended to be created by reading this material. The author assumes no liability for any errors or omissions or for how this book or its contents are used or interpreted, or for any consequences resulting directly or indirectly from the use of this book. For legal or any other advice, please consult an experienced attorney or the appropriate expert, who is aware of the specific facts of your case and is knowledgeable in the law in your jurisdiction.

Boucher Law, PC

www.boucherAI.law

www.AIRevolution.law

Northern California Office	Southern California Office
2081 Center St.	321 S Brand Blvd.
Berkeley, CA 94704	Glendale, CA 91204
(510) 838-1000	(626) 838-1000

Table of Contents

Introduction

Christopher's practice focuses on labor and employment law, and his expertise includes representing employers in a union environment, including labor negotiations, changes to existing terms and conditions of employment and the effects of those changes, and the meaning and application of labor contract provisions. He also serves as trusted counsel to employers throughout California regarding employee discipline, due process, grievance procedure issues, workplace accommodation/interactive process issues, and other labor and employment law matters.

In addition to his advocacy skills, Christopher has successfully utilized his mediation training to achieve settlements on labor and employment matters. As an experienced workplace investigator, Christopher holds the Association of Workplace Investigators Certificate Holder (AWI-CH) credential, in addition to serving as part-time faculty for the Association's Training Institute for Workplace Investigators. He is also a frequent speaker at a variety of conferences on labor and employment law topics, including legal updates and keynotes.

Prior to entering private practice, Christopher spent over a decade as a seasoned human resources executive with a broad spectrum of industry experience, including municipalities, public utilities, aviation, maritime, special districts, K-12 as well as higher education. Most notably, Christopher served as the Port of Oakland's Director of Human Resources from 2014 to 2018, where he directed the Port's human resources, labor relations, benefits, EEO, leaves and disability compliance, occupational health and safety, and workers' compensation functions.

In recognition of his human resources and legal accomplishments, Christopher was featured as one of 2016's national "Top Five Rising Stars" by Human Resource Executive magazine, and he received prominent recognitions for his accomplishments as an attorney from America's Top 50 Lawyers, MyLegalWin's Top 10 Employment Attorneys and Lifetime Honoree, Elite Lawyer, and Top Lawyer by the American Institute of Legal Advocates, which identify and highlight the accomplishments of the nation's most distinguished and skilled attorneys in all fields of practice of law.

Christopher earned a Bachelor of Arts degree from the University of California, Berkeley, and graduated *cum laude* with a Juris Doctorate degree from the Abraham Lincoln University School of Law. In addition, he received a professional certificate from Cornell University's School of Industrial and Labor Relations, and attended the Harvard Negotiation Institute at Harvard Law School. Christopher is a member of the State Bar of California and a member of the Labor and Employment Law Section of the California Lawyers Association. His clients greatly value his extensive practical human resources and labor negotiations experience, in addition to his legal skills.

Chapter One

Introducing AI

You might not have realized it, but you have likely encountered AI many times before. Not so sure? Take a moment to think back. Remember a decade or two ago when you needed customer support? You had to call in and deal with those terribly-sounding robotic Interactive Voice Response (IVR) systems and press a lot of buttons before realizing you might have reached a "dead end" in the IVR system. If you are anything like me, you probably felt trapped in a maze, like the company had no interest in ever talking to you.

Although these systems are still in use today, they have become much more sophisticated. Modern automated voice prompts guide callers through a series of menu options, streamlining call routing and enhancing efficiency in customer service operations. These systems now have a much more natural feel, thanks to added pauses and emotional inflection in each automated voice.

With the "internetization" of everything in today's world, you may even find yourself typing messages to a chatbot instead of making a phone call. Even if you do call, the system is likely much better than it was ten years ago. The triage and filtering before you get assistance from a human employee still exist, but they are undoubtedly more refined and efficient. It truly is remarkable, is it not?

What is AI?

AI is the simulation of human intelligence that exists through computer algorithms to think and act like humans. From a technical standpoint, AI consists of two key elements: data and algorithms, which allow it to study human behavior, such as learning to reason, perceiving and solving problems, making informed judgments, analyzing speech and predicting future behavior. In fact, AI is not a "new technology" per se, as it has been in existence since the 1950s, but it has significantly evolved in recent years to a much more precise degree and deployment into our everyday lives.

In some ways, AI is just a computer's ability to *life-hack,* well… life. In its essence, you might think of it as *an algorithm that leverages all of our collective experiences, thoughts, and reactions to improve decision-making* all the more. We are taught as humans through our parents, family, friends, and society. It is a vital pattern that has continued generation after generation, refining and serving as the basis for how we make decisions over time. AI learns what we have learned but without potential obstacles like emotions or biases that can cause us to make errors or poor decisions. It is essentially a computer taking human experience as a foundation from which to start, with helping us as its ultimate goal.

Naturally, some worry that AI will undermine countless jobs and cause unemployment rates to soar. Others fear it signals the beginning of the end for humanity, citing The Matrix as prophecy. While I cannot predict the future, I believe AI will follow a trajectory similar to technologies we have already come to take for granted. Remember the days before the internet, or even before computers? The initial fears and outlandish claims about these technologies often stemmed from uncertainty about their potential impact.

I firmly believe the cat is already out of the bag with AI. We progressed from dial-up internet to DSL, and now we have fiber optics, harnessing the power of light signals to transmit data at unprecedented speeds. Today, people have faster internet access on a device the size of their hand than anyone had for their home computer just 15 years ago. The world is at our fingertips in ways that no one could have conceived of 30 years ago. *Do you know anyone today who would say that we should get rid of the internet?* Probably not. *Will AI just be another iteration of technological progress that gets the same response 20 years from now?* My guess is, most likely so.

In the employment context, which will be discussed further in other chapters of this book, AI is now used to perform many of the tasks that historically are time-consuming or cumbersome to do, such as conducting job screening interviews, analyzing large amounts of data to provide analytics, automating the onboarding and benefits enrollment process for new hires, conducting extensive research, evaluating witness credibility and consistency of evidence in workplace investigations, and providing around-the-clock service to organizations big and small that rely on HR support. As with other technologies that have evolved over time, AI is sure to be (and has already become) the "next big thing" that HR will adapt to in the coming years.

The Benefits of AI in 2024

Artificial intelligence (AI) has become an important and widely used tool across various technologies and industries. While AI has existed in some form for decades, its scope and application have expanded rapidly in recent years. The National Artificial Intelligence Initiative Act of 2020 (NAIIA) defines AI as a "machine-based system that can, for a given set of human-defined objectives, make predictions, recommendations or decisions influencing real or virtual environments."[1]

Of course, there are different levels of AI, but the most advanced form closely simulates human cognition. Take Tesla's self-driving technology, for instance. Tesla prides and distinguishes itself on how Tesla cars can drive themselves. *How did they come up with that technology?* In some ways, by relying on AI. Tesla cars use AI to analyze and monitor various factors like road conditions, light changes, traffic patterns, speed and driver reactions. This technology learns from collective human experiences, continually refining its decision-making capabilities based on real-world data.

Imagine you are driving on the interstate, and a car seems to swerve into your lane. You might start panicking, thinking, *"That driver is going to sideswipe me and endanger my spouse in the passenger seat! I need to avoid them immediately,"* and swerve hard into the lane

---

[1]National Artificial Intelligence Initiative Act of 2020, Pub. L. No. 116-283, § 5002(3) (2021).

on your left without seeing that you are about to hit another vehicle. A self-driving car operates without that emotional response, which can easily override a person's sober-minded analysis. It objectively assesses the situation and determines the best decision under the circumstances, which may actually be slowing down or speeding up instead of swerving left.

Even more importantly, this technology draws on a larger perspective when making these split-second decisions. While we have two eyes that allow us to look forward, Tesla's self-driving AI assesses data from cameras on the front, back, and both sides of the car. Imagine not having to process multiple questions like, "What is to my left? What is to my right? What is behind me? What is in front of me?" sequentially, but having that information available simultaneously. While we are limited to a 180° field of vision, AI has, in many ways, a 360° view of the surroundings.

This is AI at play in real life. AI takes in large amounts of data, analyzes it for correlations and patterns, and then uses it to make informed decisions and predictions. Using the Tesla AI example, it is conceivable that the AI can predict what other drivers might do based on their driving behavior and then make informed decisions to either slow down, change lanes, or move ahead of the other vehicle *before* an accident ever occurs, making roads safer for everyone.

AI also offers many advantages. Because of its analytical capacity and ability to respond quickly, it excels at detail-oriented jobs, reducing time for data-heavy tasks, saving labor, and increasing productivity. It delivers consistent results and can potentially improve the overall service experience through personalization and timely response. Additionally, an AI-powered system is always available since AI does not need to sleep like humans do.

Whether or not we realize it, we have all encountered different forms of AI over time. It started with automation using industrial robots almost 50 years ago, which evolved into machine learning, followed by natural language processing, and now self-driving cars. The technology has come a long way, and its reliability has significantly improved in recent years. In some cases today, AI-generated language and visual content can even exceed what humans create - with the exception of this book, of course!

The Adoption of AI in American Industries

If you have spent any time considering the implications of this technology on human society, from industry to education or healthcare, you may think it has no bounds. Although this may not be literally true, it is not much of an exaggeration to come to that conclusion, especially from our current vantage point. As I mentioned earlier, this technology is revolutionary. We have already begun to see its impact, but what is perhaps the most mind-boggling is that the extent we have seen so far is barely the tip of the iceberg.

When thinking about AI and the workforce, everything boils down to one thing—enhancement. Like any tool or technology, the goal of AI is to enhance the quality of life, making processes exponentially more efficient. When considering this, I constantly come back to how AI is really no different than machinery. Rewind 200 years, and we were all riding horses. Fast forward 100 years, and we had cars. Twenty years ago, we had cars with cruise control. Now, we have self-driving cars. Just as the Industrial Revolution disrupted industries across the globe, AI will make our current way of life look wildly different in the years to come.

In many ways, AI is just a vehicle to make life better. This serves as a new baseline for humanity. With AI, we will not have to bog ourselves down with nearly as many mundane, mentally inconsequential, and time-consuming tasks as we do now. Instead, we can focus on what really matters. With all this in mind, it is easy to see why AI has become central to many of today's largest and most successful companies, including Alphabet, Apple, Microsoft, and Meta, where AI technologies are used to improve operations and enhance competition. It has already proven to be disruptive, and it is anticipated that it will become even more widespread over the next few years.

Here, we will briefly consider just a few areas where you can see AI already significantly influencing human society. Of course, the possible scope of AI's implementation across industries is not limited to the areas I'll cover here, but this will, nonetheless, provide a brief yet illustrative depiction of this phenomenon at work in our world today.[2]

Healthcare

AI is already playing a role in making medical diagnoses. The AI-based systems in place today allow you to describe the symptoms you are experiencing to a chatbot. These systems can, in turn, narrow down what you are dealing with somewhat reliably. Although there is still room for considerable improvement, for less severe illnesses like colds or the flu, it does the trick—saving both you and medical providers time and money. Additionally, by the time you actually see the provider, it speeds up the diagnostic process.

---

[2] "Our Early-Adopters Index Examines How Corporate America Is Deploying AI," *The Economist*, July 1, 2023, https://www.economist.com/business/2023/06/25/our-early-adopters-index-examines-how-corporate-america-is-deploying-ai.

On a more advanced level, AI machines are not only learning to perform surgeries but also to perform them with a much higher degree of precision and efficiency than human hands can achieve. With AI, we no longer need to rely on humans to make all decisions and risk human error. Instead, AI builds on a foundation laid by *decades* of human experience and data.

Business

Machine learning algorithms are being integrated into analytics and customer relationship management platforms to uncover information on how to better serve customers. As mentioned earlier, chatbots are often used to provide immediate customer support, but that is only the beginning. AI integration is expected to have far-reaching consequences well into the future, revolutionizing product design and disrupting existing business models across the board.

Education

AI is already dramatically enhancing how we interact with education, both on the teacher and learner side. With AI, different learners can get varying levels of training tailored directly to them with minimal friction.

For example, if you are exceptionally capable and can ace basic training at your new job within an hour, an AI-based system designed to test and detect your abilities would allow you to customize your learning experience. Instead of undergoing a standard five-day training, AI can help you decide where you need to focus more time and when to advance to the next phase.

This individualized approach not only saves the employer a week's worth of time but also provides a stimulating start that meets you right where you are. The result? Your employer benefits from efficient training, and you enjoy a more satisfying learning experience.

The point is this: AI allows organizations of all kinds, from schools to workplaces, to move away from a cookie-cutter approach and tailor the learning experience to each person - saving everyone time and money along the way.

Banking and Finance

As is true across many other industries, AI has revolutionized customer service in the financial sector. In many ways, this is due to the fact that banks often close at 5 PM and are not open on weekends, which is simply not conducive to our increasingly digital and global world, where many transactions are conducted "after hours." Fortunately, AI now provides 24/7 customer service and transaction processing, irrespective of brick-and-mortar operating hours.

AI is doing so much more than this, though – it also plays a crucial role in fraud detection. Instances of fraud that could take a team of people years to figure out can now be identified in minutes, if not seconds, with AI. Constantly monitoring activities to catch fraudulent actions in real-time, AI is like a vehicle that *never needs to stop.* In fact, when you receive a call or text message from your bank alerting you of fraudulent activities on your credit card, it is likely that the AI algorithm has detected unusual activities and is seeking to stop the transaction as it is happening to protect your account.

Additionally, AI is transforming personal finance applications, such as Intuit Mint or TurboTax, by collecting personal data and providing financial advice. This is not to mention that today, artificial intelligence software performs much of the trading on Wall Street.

Legal

Although there is clearly still a way to go, the level to which AI is already changing the world of law is fascinating. Traditionally, you would have to rely on lawyers with years of training and education to conduct very traditional research that could take days and a considerable amount of resources. We are now seeing that AI has visibly sped up this process with its ability to analyze, interpret, and draft various legal texts and documents at a speed and scale that far surpasses human capabilities.

In addition to this, I believe that AI will greatly expand the public's access to the law. Unfortunately, there is a massive barrier to entry for obtaining solid legal advice and representation. My estimation is that

AI will reduce the cost factors that contribute to this barrier of entry. Although this is still yet to be seen in any meaningful way, it is on the horizon of becoming a reality. Of course, this technology will never replace an attorney who can provide legal advice or representation, but it will enhance their capabilities by reducing overall legal costs while allowing attorneys to provide more timely service.

On top of this, AI-powered legal research platforms often incorporate advanced natural language processing capabilities, allowing people to search for legal information using plain language. This will continue to democratize access to legal knowledge, making it easier for those without prior experience dealing with the law to navigate complex legal issues and understand their rights and obligations.

At our firm, Boucher Law, PC, we happily experiment with AI. Specifically, we have deployed AI in the areas of legal research, analytics, and some basic drafting, as these are areas that traditionally require a considerable amount of time for attorneys. For example, a novel or complex legal question used to take human hours to perform research at a law library, and now, AI can generate a "first glance" response within minutes, allowing attorneys to verify the sources of information and make a final determination in a less time-consuming fashion.

AI can also draft memorandums while incorporating legal and case law citations in minutes, which allows attorneys to provide legal advice and services far more efficiently than we have been able to do in the past. So, while I am not sure exactly what AI applications lie ahead of us, we are excited to try something new. I strongly believe that having this open mind gives us a strong advantage as this technology moves forward and we partner with employers along the way.

In addition, our firm has formed a dedicated AI Practice Group with a team of attorneys and consultants who can provide advice and counsel on legal and practical issues related to the adaptation of AI in the workplace. Given our team's decades of experience serving as both general counsel and in labor and employment law, we are able to assist companies, nonprofits, and government entities in areas such as commercial transactions involving AI, tort liability and litigation, data protection and privacy issues, intellectual property and technology, ethical considerations, and implementing AI in the workplace.

Overall, while the journey of integrating AI into the legal industry is just beginning, the potential benefits are immense. By embracing AI, we can make the law more accessible, efficient, and equitable for everyone.

Entertainment and Media

In the entertainment sector, businesses use AI for targeted advertising, content recommendations, distribution, fraud detection, and content creation. Among other uses, AI can also create new images and videos of an actor without their involvement - and in a manner so precise that the audience cannot tell the difference. As we will discuss in later chapters of this book, this has become a hotly contested issue involving creators' rights and ethical concerns.

Furthermore, deepfakes are images, videos, or audio recordings that have been manipulated using AI to appear real but are actually false. Deepfakes can replace faces, manipulate facial expressions, synthesize faces, and synthesize speech. They can make it look like someone is saying or doing something they did not actually do or say, causing significant privacy and misappropriation concerns.

Meanwhile, automated journalism helps newsrooms streamline media workflows, reducing time, costs, and complexity. Like any other office, newsrooms use AI to automate routine tasks, such as data entry and proofreading. However, the manner in which journalists can reliably use ChatGPT and other generative AI tools to shape reporting remains to be seen, particularly given these programs' potential to generate misinformation.

Software Coding and IT

AI can produce application code based on natural language prompts. It is also being used to automate many IT processes, such as data entry, fraud detection, customer service, predictive maintenance, and security. AI is making significant strides in enhancing productivity and efficiency across the board.

In recent years, AI has greatly influenced software development by improving code quality, automating tasks, and enhancing project management. AI assists developers in various ways, such as automating repetitive tasks, generating similar strings of code to free up time for more complex and creative programming, offering coding suggestions and auto-completing lines of code, detecting bugs and troubleshooting issues, speeding up the development cycle, and leveraging historical data, real-time information, and algorithms to forecast trends, identify patterns, and predict future outcomes.

For example, AI systems can analyze historical project data and patterns to predict potential roadblocks, estimate project timelines, and optimize resource allocation. Additionally, natural language processing (NLP) models can convert plain language descriptions into executable code, enabling quicker experimentation and implementation of ideas.

Security

AI is being applied successfully to various aspects of cybersecurity, including anomaly detection, solving the false-positive problem, and conducting behavioral threat analytics. Although AI has been used in certain industries for security and threat assessment for decades, it is now being deployed on a much larger scale. Many organizations today use machine learning in security information, event management software, and other related areas to detect anomalies and identify suspicious activities that indicate threats. For example, CrowdStrike is a company that does exactly just that.

In today's deployment, AI is able to continuously scan and monitor workplaces for concerns such as weapons, theft, and other illegal activities. Through the use of facial recognition, AI can "spot" individuals within seconds and alert the appropriate authorities. Furthermore, AI robots can now roam around and monitor workplaces, making it safer for security personnel to have a "partner" without risking human life. *One of the key benefits so far?* By analyzing camera feeds with a high level of reliability and precision, AI is able to generate alerts of new and emerging attacks much quicker than any human or previous technological iteration ever has before.

Manufacturing and Construction

Industrial robots that were once programmed to perform a single task and operate separately from human workers are increasingly functioning as "cobots": smaller robots that can multitask and collaborate with humans, taking on more parts of the job. Today, robots possess great dexterity and mobility, allowing them to navigate places such as warehouses, manufacturing plants, and construction sites. The "hands" of these robots can perform tasks similar to humans, including lifting, pulling, pushing, bending, assembling, and manipulating fine objects, enabling them to process and assemble with both speed and accuracy.

One particularly interesting example of this is found in the construction field, where workers can use AI-backed apps to identify the presence of water or gas pipes before digging a trench by simply *asking* if the ground they are about to dig is safe to proceed with. Similarly, AI can provide construction blueprints by scanning a room, analyzing GPS coordinates, and pulling historical building permits - offering instantaneous insights that may not have been possible in the past.

Transportation

Beyond operating autonomous vehicles, AI is already being used to manage traffic, predict flight delays, and make ocean shipping safer and more efficient. For example, AI can analyze weather predictions, determine the best routes, handle delays and rebooking, and find the "best path forward" in case of unforeseen issues.

AI-powered systems can optimize traffic flow and reduce congestion, which can help prevent accidents. Computer vision camera systems can capture license plate numbers, locations, dates, and times, and feed the data into a central server.

In supply chains, AI is replacing traditional methods of forecasting demand and predicting disruptions—a trend accelerated by COVID-19, which caught many companies off guard regarding the effects of a global pandemic on the supply and demand of goods.

Lastly, AI can even help warehouses reduce operations costs, increase safety, and optimize delivery routes to save time and fuel. AI can also help warehouses better handle potential delays through predictive analysis.

The Future of AI

Now that we have seen how this technology is beginning to permeate all aspects of industry and human society, the question becomes how we transition *the entire workforce* to adapt to AI – just as we did with computers a couple of decades ago and the internet more recently.

I believe that this technology is ready for *"prime time"* in many ways, but are the American or global economies prepared for the shift? The analytics suggest that the writing is on the wall. A LinkedIn report released in August of 2023 states that 44% of executives plan to increase their use of AI, and 47% believe it will increase overall productivity.[3] Clearly, we are only witnessing the infancy of this paradigm-shifting technology, and we need to position *everyone* accordingly.

Is ChatGPT Here to Stay?

In his 2023 essay titled *The Age of AI Has Begun*, Bill Gates identified the technology behind ChatGPT as one of the two most groundbreaking he has witnessed in his lifetime.[4] The other is the graphical user interface (GUI), which is what allows people using computers and similar devices to interact with the software through graphical icons and visual indicators, as opposed to text-based interfaces, typed command labels, or text navigation. Similarly to the massive changes brought by GUI, Gates believes that the

---

[3]LinkedIn Economic Graph, *Future of Work Report: AI – August 2023.* LinkedIn, August 2023, https://economicgraph.linkedin.com/content/dam/me/economicgraph/en-us/PDF/future-of-work-report-ai-august-2023.pdf.

[4]Bill Gates, "The Age of AI Has Begun," *Gates Notes*, March 21, 2023, https://www.gatesnotes.com/The-Age-of-AI-Has-Begun.

technology underlying ChatGPT will fundamentally reorient entire industries.

The fact that this statement comes from none other than the "Sultan of Software" himself carries immense weight - and it is easy to see his point. AI-powered chatbots have already taken over many workplace functions, such as reception, customer service, online chat, and queries. While there are still some limitations, the technology is advancing every day. Tools like AI chatbots can make creating, summarizing, and translating text easier, allowing human workers to revise, edit, and make necessary corrections and customizations at an unprecedented speed. Therefore, there is no doubt in my mind that chatbots are here to stay.

Practical Tips for Adopting AI

For employers exploring the possibility of implementing ChatGPT in the workplace (or those who have deployed AI already), here are a few key points to keep in mind:

- **Determine** whether employees are allowed (or encouraged) to use ChatGPT or similar tools and whether there should be any restrictions or limitations on the use of these tools in the course of their work.
- **Comply** with any state or local laws requiring audits or notice if using ChatGPT or other automated decision tools in the hiring process.
- **Understand** the legal risks of using ChatGPT in the workplace, such as:
  - The potential employer liability based on the inherent bias and limitations of AI, depending on the data on which the tool is trained;
  - The possibility that ChatGPT will provide inaccurate responses; and
  - The potential for disclosure of trade secrets and other confidential information when engaging with ChatGPT.

The Benefits of Adopting AI

Consider this: Implementing AI in the workplace is similar to how word processing used to exist as an entire department until companies started introducing computers to the office. This technology made word processing take a fraction of the time and effort. People no longer had to write things by hand or dictate for someone to transcribe. With the advent of the internet, you could log onto a computer, type (or speak) out an email, and send it within a matter of minutes.

I believe we are headed for a similar transformation in HR. In the coming years, AI will likely become much more expansive and accessible - and it will not just be limited to the office. There are many AI technologies that are app-driven, enabling even field employees to get what they need simply by using their smartphones.

The Drawbacks of Adopting AI

As I have mentioned several times throughout this book already, there are overwhelming benefits to using AI. However, it is crucial to discuss the potential drawbacks associated with its use, as well. An honest forecast of what this exceptional technology can mean for human society must include a fair assessment of the potential downsides.

AI is so new and potentially game-changing that many people are understandably wary of it. The biggest hesitation surrounds its impact on jobs. Many are worried they will see their pay slashed because AI is doing half of their job or that they will find themselves out of work entirely. This anxiety is the biggest factor that will determine whether employees embrace AI, and it will likely serve as the basis for what HR needs to consider as AI becomes more integrated into companies.

Beyond job loss, there are other considerations. These issues might not be as visible, given the economic benefits AI may enable, but they are real and worth engaging with. COVID-19 gave us a sampling of it. In some ways, AI has already impacted the workforce more gradually than we might realize. We have experienced increased levels of loneliness and the erosion of social life, especially when paired with robotics. Keeping a close eye on the way that AI influences the way we interact with each other will be pivotal in our ability to make thoughtful and informed decisions about how we create a future aided by artificial intelligence.

Closing Thoughts

As with any new technology, it is crucial to balance the potential that AI holds for transforming the world around us with a thoughtful consideration of its potential disadvantages. It is clear how significantly AI can enhance our efficiency, productivity, and personalization in the workplace.

By making our routine tasks a second thought, workers can look toward a future where a greater part of the day is spent completing work that requires ideation, innovation, and creativity. Even so, we must continually address concerns of displacement, bias, and isolation. To do this, employers will need to be proactive in their approach to addressing these challenges by implementing fair policies, providing training, and ensuring the proper use of AI.

As we continue to embrace this AI revolution, we must foster a world where these tools *complement and enhance* human capabilities rather than replace them altogether. By doing so, we can harness the full potential of AI – and ourselves – all while safeguarding the well-being of each individual in the workplace. The future of AI is promising. **The future of AI** ***is already here.***

Chapter Two

The Practical Use Of AI In the HR Profession

The landscape of human resources (HR) is ever-changing, and it continues to evolve rapidly. It is no surprise that technology as innovative as AI is emerging with the potential to transform the field. Whether by streamlining operations, assisting with administrative tasks, offering insights, or empowering employees to access their benefits, the implications of AI provide overwhelming benefits to those who can implement and refine their use of the technology in their every day.

Jeanne Meister discusses this in further detail in her article *The Future of Work: The Intersection of Artificial Intelligence and Human Resources.*[5] This piece

---

[5]Jeanne Meister, "The Future of Work: The Intersection of Artificial Intelligence and Human Resources," *Forbes*, March 1, 2017.

of writing is over six years old, but nonetheless, it is great reading, and I heartily recommend it to anyone looking to take a deep dive into the topic. But before you do, let us do some of our exploring at the crossroads of AI and HR …

AI Use Cases in HR Settings

The use cases for AI abound across industries and the arena of life. As I have mentioned, AI is already being used in several industries and parts of society. Today, 99% of Fortune 500 companies are already using AI.[6] Honing in on HR specifically, the same holds true. In Eightfold AI's report *The Future of Work: Intelligent by Design*[7], the majority of the 250 HR leaders surveyed said they are already using AI across HR functions, such as:

---

https://www.forbes.com/sites/jeannemeister/2017/03/01/the-future-of-work-the-intersection-of-artificial-intelligence-and-human-resources/.

[6]Rohit Shewale, "How Many Companies Use AI (Latest Data)," *DemandSage*, March 13, 2024, https://www.demandsage.com/companies-using-ai/.

[7]Eightfold AI, *The Future of Work: Intelligent by Design: Eightfold AI's 2022 Talent Survey*, https://eightfold.ai/wp-content/uploads/2022_Talent_Survey.pdf.

- Employee records management (78%)
- Payroll processing and benefits administration (77%)
- Recruitment and hiring (73%)
- Performance management (72%)
- Onboarding new employees (69%)

In terms of future use, 92 percent of HR leaders intend to increase their AI use in at least one area of HR, including:

- Performance management (43%)
- Payroll processing and benefits administration (42%)
- Recruitment and hiring (41%)
- Onboarding new employees (40%)
- Employee records management (39%).

Of those surveyed, most reported that they plan to increase their usage in the next 12 to 18 months. In fact, a stunning 80 percent of global HR professionals believe that AI will be a tool to help them with their work over the next five years.[8]

For example, in the area of HR operations, AI can assist with:

Employee Self-Service

AI-driven HR chatbots and virtual assistants can handle routine HR inquiries 24/7, answering questions about benefits, employee leave, and company policy. This frees up time for HR to focus on strategic tasks, while employees get instant answers whenever they need them.

Benefits Administration

One example of HR chatbots at play is in benefits administration, where a 24/7 service center can dramatically improve employees' lives. Imagine a new employee sorting out their benefits. A chatbot like ChatGPT, equipped with the correct data, could save

---

[8]Hari Srinivasan, "Reimagining Hiring and Learning with the Power of AI," *LinkedIn Talent Blog*, LinkedIn, https://www.linkedin.com/business/talent/blog/talent-acquisition/reimagining-hiring-and-learning-with-power-of-ai.

the employee valuable time. Rather than waiting until the next day to talk with someone from HR after coming up with questions with their spouse while working through the paperwork together, they could ask the company chatbot directly—at any hour of the day.

In another example, evaluating which medical plan to stay on or whether their go-to dentist is covered by the new policy are just a few practical tasks that ChatGPT can perform. Additionally, it would enhance processes like open enrollment, speeding up the paperwork considerably. Clearly, empowering employees with the ability to self-service is a win-win situation for both the company and the employee.

Leave Requests

Another area where an AI chatbot could efficiently provide answers and offer interactive support for employees is in managing leave requests. Whether for baby bonding, medical treatment, or care for a family member, requesting leave tends to be a very stressful process for most employees. It is not uncommon for questions like, "When do I need to return to work?" or "When does my medical coverage transition to COBRA benefits?" to arise during this time.

By providing employees with this information at their fingertips at all hours, chatbots can alleviate this stress and enhance the overall employee experience. Additionally, with various leaves such as the Family Medical Leave Act, state and local leave statutes, and other leaves specific to childbirth, baby bonding, family care, and workers' compensation all at play, AI can effectively integrate the various leaves to provide accurate information for employees to plan for time off.

In other instances, AI can also detect fraud or leave abuse patterns by analyzing employee leave data and comparing it against trends in the workgroup, holidays, and other types of time off. For larger organizations, this is a valuable tool to monitor and enhance productivity, as well as to ensure consistency in leave administration across the organization.

Hiring and Onboarding

AI can provide a customized onboarding experience for each employee based on their position. By tailoring training, benefits enrollment, and debriefing according to individual responses, the process becomes much more seamless and less of a "cookie cutter" approach. Additionally, AI can assist in the hiring process at key points, reducing the time HR professionals spend on menial tasks and allowing them to focus on selecting the perfect candidate for any role.

Talent Acquisition

AI dramatically enhances talent acquisition by producing a shortlist of candidates after conducting searches, sourcing candidates, contacting them, automating the screening interview, and ranking them. This task, which could take a recruiter or an entire team at least a week to complete, is expedited by AI tremendously.

The benefits of AI in the hiring process do not stop there, either. This technology can conduct interviews, either independently or in conjunction with a human, score the quality of responses algorithmically, and assess how they match the job qualifications. AI can also analyze candidate skills and aptitudes, administer testing, and use chatbots to accelerate the hiring and communication process, thereby completing the recruitment cycle seamlessly and expeditiously.

Job Descriptions

AI can generate job descriptions based on the experiences of employers, industry standards, and best practices in the field. What is more, AI can do this in *a fraction* of the time that the same task would take a person, often within a single minute.

The added benefits of using AI-generated job descriptions can include consistency (ensuring that all job postings have the same level of detail and quality), inclusivity (by flagging potentially biased language by suggesting alternative phrasing), and optimizing job descriptions for search engines, making them more likely to appear in job search results.

So, while it still takes a human to make any necessary determinations pertaining to the quality of the description in the end, it speeds that process up *considerably*. Yet again, the key here does not lie in replacing the human effort but in *enhancing it*.

Data Analytics, Workforce Planning, & Retention

Perhaps most interestingly, AI can analyze large volumes of HR data to identify trends, patterns, and insights related to workforce planning, employee engagement, attrition, and diversity metrics. This comprehensive analysis can reveal key information about a company's workforce, such as which employees should receive raises, who might be dissatisfied with their work-life balance, and predict which roles might need to be filled in the next year based on current workforce skills, industry trends, attrition rates, and company growth plans.

By analyzing workforce data and comparing it against historical trends, AI can determine potential "flight risks" in different departments and across positions, allowing organizations to address issues before they become problematic. Additionally, AI can recommend compensation adjustments based on performance data, helping to retain employees whose performance warrants recognition.

Labor Relations and Compensation

In areas like labor relations negotiations, AI can conduct much of the research on comparable benefits, compensation, and organizations—traditionally known as a salary survey. Beyond just doing the footwork, AI can also aggregate the data, making it effectively digestible to the relevant people or teams by analyzing market data, employee performance, and other relevant factors. This provides insights for determining competitive compensation packages and recommending performance-based incentives and recognition programs.

Performance Management

When it comes to performance management, AI leaves emotions aside and assesses the raw data objectively – assuming that the data it is given is accurate and fair. For example, an AI assistant could identify shortfalls, determine successful employee profiles, and compare performance against these profiles. Furthermore, it can recommend time-saving measures, provide metrics to measure success, and suggest ways to improve performance across the board.

Beyond these applications, AI can serve as a key tool in the new era of "quiet quitting" by providing significant insight into the workforce and alerting HR and management if it detects a lack of engagement in certain workgroups, allowing proactive steps to be taken for performance management and retention purposes. By tracking and analyzing employee performance, AI provides comprehensive reports highlighting workforce strengths, areas for improvement, and progress over time, leading to even greater transparency and fairness in the evaluation process.

Coaching And Talent Development

AI can provide coaching in various ways, including career coaching, learning and development, performance feedback, and identifying potential opportunities for promotion and retention. While people can be more sensitive to criticism from those close to them, AI can act as a substitute, offering private, objective coaching and concrete suggestions for improvement. On top of optimizing quality and efficiency, this approach can be more constructive and less awkward than traditional manager-employee meetings.

A Cautionary Word About Limited Thinking

Because AI is a technology with such far-reaching ramifications, it is important that we do not view it through a segmented lens, as easy as it may be to do. Thinking AI will fix productivity in one area may be true, but it may leave you missing the forest for the trees. In fact, a survey conducted by McKinsey's Global shows that 27 percent of HR respondents reported their AI adoption resulted in a cost reduction of *less than 10 percent,* while 23 percent reported an average revenue increase of 6 to 10 percent.[9] This is not

---

[9]Arif Cam, Michael Chui, and Bryce Hall, "Global AI Survey: AI Proves Its Worth, but Few Scale Impact," *McKinsey & Company*, November 22, 2019, https://www.mckinsey.com/featured-insights/artificial-intelligence/global-ai-survey-ai-proves-its-worth-but-few-scale-impact.

an insignificant savings, but it likely does not quite live up to the hype business leaders were sold.

My advice? Take a holistic approach to implementing AI for all of society, your enterprise, and in every way possible. I like this analogy: Imagine you are building or remodeling a house. It is easy to take an old approach. First, you think, "We should just change out the kitchen counters." Next thing you know, you end up hating the paint and decide to redo it. People are almost always chasing one thing or another at any given time.

Taking this approach means you will have a much higher probability of your house coming out looking a bit strange because you made so many decisions at different times, so nothing matches. Some things are modern; others are out of date. Some things are awkwardly placed; others fit like a glove. Doing the same when it comes to using AI will yield similar outcomes.

Remember, AI is ultimately just a tool. Have a clear plan when implementing it. Even if you cannot afford to remodel the entire house, approach the small tasks you can with a comprehensive perspective and objective. Use the principles of kaizen, which is a Japanese term meaning change for the better or continuous improvement.[10] This way, when you do get around to checking other things off your to-do list, whenever that may be, you will have a beautiful and sturdy house. This comprehensive approach has countless benefits.

Most importantly, by intentionally exercising a balance of innovation and risk management, organizations can avoid falling into the trap of spinning their wheels chasing the latest trend.

---

[10] As will be further explained in Chapter 7, kaizen is a Japanese business philosophy that concerns the processes that continuously improve operations and involve all employees. Kaizen sees improvement in productivity as a gradual and methodical process involving all employees from the CEO to the assembly line workers.

Chapter Three

How AI is Impacting the Workforce

AI is rapidly making an impact on the workforce. Organizations that have adopted AI are actively managing data quality, availability, security, and governance frameworks to ensure success. They are building teams with technical expertise, and this is where HR comes in to establish ethical standards to ensure fairness, accountability, and transparent practices to build trust with the workforce. This is perhaps the most critical component to ensure the long-term success and viability of implementing AI in the workforce.

Are Your Employees Embracing AI?

AI is no longer a futuristic concept; it is at the heart of today's workplace transformation. Despite 36 percent of UK and US employees using AI on a weekly basis at work, less than a quarter of companies provide any guidance for their workers on how they should be harnessing the technology, according to new research by Asana.[11] Roughly half (52%) of knowledge workers anticipate that AI will positively impact their work, and more than one-third (36%) are already harnessing AI's capabilities in their roles at least weekly. However, despite recognizing AI's potential, challenges remain.

On average, nearly one-third (29%) of employees believe their jobs are replaceable by AI. Given the uncertainties that could impact their jobs, it is understandable that employees are hesitant about the change. The only way to ensure success is by thoughtfully implementing AI with a "human touch," fostering trust and collaboration, and helping employees learn new skills to work more efficiently with the help of AI going forward.

---

[11] Alicia Raeburn, "The Reality of AI in Today's Workplace (New Research)," *Asana*, September 15, 2023, https://asana.com/resources/state-of-ai-research-takeaways.

Can AI Replace Human Jobs?

While the adoption of AI continues to grow, a common concern is: Will AI take away our jobs? The short answer is "not necessarily." The truth is, groundbreaking advancements in AI technology, such as ChatGPT, have already changed the labor market in America. According to OpenAI researchers, ChatGPT's creators, this technology could affect 19 percent of U.S. jobs, with around 80 percent of American workers potentially feeling its impact.[12] Furthermore, McKinsey & Company estimated that between 400 million and 800 million jobs could be lost to automation by 2030 – and that was in 2017, years before ChatGPT came onto the scene.[13]

---

[12]Tyna Eloundou, Sam Manning, Pamela Mishkin, and Daniel Rock, "GPTs Are GPTs: An Early Look at the Labor Market Impact Potential of Large Language Models," *arXiv*, first submitted March 17, 2023, last revised August 21, 2023, https://arxiv.org/abs/2303.10130.

[13]James Manyika et al, "Jobs Lost, Jobs Gained: What the Future of Work Will Mean for Jobs, Skills, and Wages," *McKinsey Global Institute*, November 28, 2017, https://www.mckinsey.com/featured-insights/future-of-work/jobs-lost-jobs-gained-what-the-future-of-work-will-mean-for-jobs-skills-and-wages.

Over time, AI is expected to automate more tasks and enhance human functions, enabling employees to work more efficiently and freeing up time for more engaging tasks. This shift could move the workforce into new, more fulfilling roles, much like how various tools, from computers to heavy equipment, have historically allowed us to accomplish greater feats than ever before. In fact, as AI takes some of the mundane tasks out of workers' days, particularly in knowledge-work roles, experts anticipate that many jobs will become more sophisticated and creative. Productivity could spike, too, as employees transition time-consuming minutiae to machines, changing fundamental job descriptions and increasing output quality.

Jobs Most at Risk

Considering Pew's research[14], sectors with jobs at the most risk of AI or automation replacement are:

- Transportation and material moving

---

[14]Rakesh Kochhar, "Which U.S. Workers Are More Exposed to AI on Their Jobs?" *Pew Research Center*, July 26, 2023, https://www.pewresearch.org/social-trends/2023/07/26/which-u-s-workers-are-more-exposed-to-ai-on-their-jobs/.

- Sales and sales-related roles
- Production
- Office and administrative support
- Food preparation
- Business and financial operations
- Art, design, entertainment, sports, and media
- Building, grounds cleaning, and maintenance
- Personal care and service operations
- Protective service operations

The primary reason for the job loss is efficiency. AI systems can often perform tasks faster, more accurately, and at a lower cost than human workers, making routine, repetitive tasks particularly vulnerable. On the other hand, because AI can handle tasks like data entry and simple transactions, it allows human workers to focus on more challenging tasks that require deeper insight, empathy, or decision-making.

While AI's capabilities continue to advance, certain job roles remain inherently resistant to automation. Fields such as teaching, writing, law, social work, medicine, therapy, and management rely on human expertise and intuition. Professions that require creativity, communication, judgment, empathy, strategic thinking, and human interaction are less susceptible to displacement by AI. Similarly, jobs involving manual work and skilled labor are minimally exposed to AI disruption.

Jobs That May Emerge from AI

The Forbes Technology Council predicts new jobs that AI could create, as well as current specialties that may become even more in demand with the rise of AI[15], including:

- AI Trainer And Operator
- Sentiment Analyzer
- Content Creator
- AI-Generated Work Auditor
- AI Prediction Analyzer
- AI Input And Output Manager
- AI Integration Specialist

---

[15]Forbes Technology Council, "20 New and Enhanced Roles AI Could Create," *Forbes*, July 6, 2023, https://www.forbes.com/councils/forbestechcouncil/2023/07/06/20-new-and-enhanced-roles-ai-could-create/.

- AI Compliance Manager
- AI Ethicist
- AI Applications Developer
- AI Instructors
- Language Ingestion Optimizer
- AI Personality Designer
- AI Security Engineer

This means that, despite concerns about job displacement, many studies suggest that AI has the potential to create even more jobs than it replaces. The World Economic Forum, for example, predicts that while AI may replace around 85 million jobs by 2025, it will also create approximately 97 million new roles.[16]

Robots in the Workplace

As much as it seems like a reality far into the future, robots are now working among human workers. In fact, robots are now working alongside human

---

[16]Amanda Russo, "Recession and Automation Changes Our Future of Work, But There Are Jobs Coming, Report Says," *World Economic Forum*, October 20, 2020, https://www.weforum.org/press/2020/10/recession-and-automation-changes-our-future-of-work-but-there-are-jobs-coming-report-says-52c5162fce/.

workers. For decades, specialized robots, such as those on assembly lines moving pieces of metal repeatedly, have worked with people. Today, AI-powered robots have become common in the workforce, performing highly repetitive tasks, manual or dangerous tasks, and tasks requiring a high degree of consistency.

Why are organizations deploying robots? Robots have the ability to enhance speed and efficiency, improve precision and accuracy, leverage cognitive abilities for certain decisions, adapt to new tasks, and achieve physical strength and endurance beyond human capability. When deployed appropriately, they make a great partner to employees.

Creating Efficiency and Enhancing Work-Life Balance with Use of AI

By leveraging AI, organizations can introduce new approaches that optimize productivity and empower employees to have a healthier work-life balance, such as:

1.) Task Automation

AI can automate repetitive and time-consuming tasks, freeing up valuable hours that can be utilized for other higher-value responsibilities.

2.) Time Management

AI can analyze data and patterns to provide intelligent insights on time management. By analyzing individual work patterns, preferences, and priorities, AI can help employees allocate their time more effectively, leading to increased productivity.

3.) Personalized Workflows

AI algorithms can learn from individual work habits, tailoring workflows to suit each employee's strengths and preferences.

4.) Decision Support

AI-powered virtual assistants can provide real-time support, helping employees access information, schedule tasks, and prioritize activities. This allows employees to make more informed decisions, leading to better outcomes.

5.) Empowering Remote Work

AI tools facilitate remote work by enabling seamless collaboration, communication, and document management. With video conferencing, virtual collaboration platforms, and AI-driven project management tools, employees can work flexibly, reducing commute time and enhancing work-life integration.

6.) Increased Well-being and Work-Life Integration

AI can help build a work environment that prioritizes employee well-being by reminding employees to take breaks, encouraging physical activity, promoting mindfulness, and recommending wellness activities to foster a healthier and more balanced lifestyle.

Adapting the Workforce to AI

Implementing AI in the workplace involves thoughtful planning, responsible integration, and clear communication with employees. Here are four key steps to ensure a successful and positive AI implementation:

1.) Thoughtful Integration

Integrate AI thoughtfully. Transparent communication with employees about the changes fosters a smooth transition, including any potential for loss of jobs and organizational restructure that may result from the implementation of AI.

2.) Ethical AI Implementation

Prioritize ethics and fairness by auditing AI systems regularly with leadership support.

3.) Upskilling and Reskilling Initiatives

Invest in upskilling and reskilling programs to prepare employees for an AI-enabled future. This may include a combination of in-house training, partnering with universities and other educational providers, as well as on-the-job training as new technologies are deployed.

4.) Collaborative AI-Human Workflows

Foster collaboration between AI systems and human workers to maximize potential. This way, humans can focus on higher-value tasks while AI complements their abilities.

Recognizing the shift to AI tools such as ChatGPT, training the workforce to adapt to AI is crucial for success. By thoughtfully integrating AI, prioritizing ethics, investing in employee upskilling, and embracing collaborative AI-human workflows, organizations can create a future workforce where AI enhances human capabilities and elevates the workforce to perform at its peak.

Developing Soft Skills

In the context of the U.S. workforce, soft skills are often underestimated, but as AI becomes more proficient at technical tasks, there will be an increasing demand for workers with strong interpersonal skills. According to a report from the Pew Research Center, about one in five U.S. workers have jobs with key tasks that are more likely to be aided or replaced by AI.[17]

---

[17]Kochhar, "Which U.S. Workers Are More Exposed to AI on Their Jobs?"

The findings, based on an analysis of federal data, indicate that jobs relying on analytical skills like critical thinking, writing, science, and math tend to be more exposed to this emerging technology. Interestingly, workers in these industries are more likely to believe AI will help rather than harm their jobs, according to Pew.

The Top 9 Soft Skills

1. Empathy
2. Emotional intelligence
3. Sociability
4. Leadership
5. Creativity
6. Mental flexibility
7. Analytical thinking
8. Personal efficiency
9. Teamwork

Adapting Your Workforce to AI

Adapting your workforce to AI will not be a simple task. It involves building employees' trust in the technology and giving them the confidence to develop new skills. However, by creating a strong culture around AI and providing your employees with the right training, education, and mentorship, your organization will be well on its way to becoming an early adopter.

Bonus Resources

3 Keys to Prepare the Workforce for AI Integration

1.) **Educate** employees about the technological changes AI will bring and build a culture of positivity around the technology.

2.) **Prepare** employees for AI re-skilling and up-skilling by encouraging a "growth mindset" in which they learn to welcome challenges. This includes informing them about how developing AI skills will set them up for career advancement.

3.) **Identify** AI use cases that will reduce time waste, mundane, repetitive tasks, and tasks that tend to result in human error.

Chapter Four

Labor & Bargaining Issues Involving AI

Labor and bargaining issues in the context of AI implementation present a captivating blend of law, ethics, and workforce dynamics. In this chapter, we will delve into an intriguing case study: the 2023 labor strikes in Hollywood. This real-world example underscores the pressing need for ethical AI practices and forward-thinking policies that safeguard workers' and employers' interests while embracing the possibilities of this new technology. Throughout this discussion, we will unpack key legal frameworks, explore emerging trends, and consider practical insights for navigating the intricate terrain of AI and employment law.

The National Labor Relations Act and Employer's Obligations to Bargain Impacts of AI

Under the National Labor Relations Act (NLRA), unions and employers must bargain in good faith about "wages, hours, and other conditions of employment," otherwise referred to as "mandatory" subjects of bargaining.[18] Therefore, the use of AI in the workplace presents additional challenges for employers with a unionized workforce, as they have an obligation to bargain collectively with a union about certain workplace changes deemed mandatory subjects of bargaining.[19] Additionally, an employer must bargain with the union about the decision to take a particular action. This type of bargaining is commonly referred to as "decision bargaining."

Decision bargaining relates to decisions to change business operations where the changes do not alter the scope or nature of the business, and labor costs are a

---

[18]National Labor Relations Act, 29 U.S.C. §§ 151-169.

[19]*Allied Chemical & Alkali Workers, Local Union No. 1 v. Pittsburgh Plate Glass Co.*, 404 U.S. 157 (1971).

significant reason for making the changes. Two Supreme Court decisions provide the framework for analyzing whether an employer must bargain about prospective changes in its business operations, such as subcontracting, introducing automation, relocating work, and partially closing a business.[20] Essentially, employers must bargain about the effects of changes to business operations that will affect terms and conditions of employment, including automating or making technology changes.[21] In contrast, employers are generally *not* required to bargain prior to making core managerial decisions pertaining to the operation of the business. These matters are generally referred to as "permissive" subjects of bargaining.

Nonetheless, employers are required to bargain about the effects of major operation changes that will affect the terms and conditions of employment. This type of bargaining is commonly referred to as "effects bargaining." With regards to effects bargaining,

---

[20]*Fibreboard Paper Products Corp. v. NLRB*, 379 U.S. 203 (1964); *First National Maintenance Corp. v. NLRB*, 452 U.S. 666 (1981).
[21]*Columbia Tribune Publ'g Co.*, 201 N.L.R.B. 538 (1973).

employers must give the union the opportunity to bargain in a "meaningful manner and at a meaningful time" about the effects of changes in business operations, even when they need not bargain about the decision to make those changes.[22] To satisfy the effects bargaining obligation, the employer must both:[23]

- Give adequate notice of the decision about changes in business operations.
- Bargain over any effects of the changes in business operations, as the union requests.

The effect of automation on a bargaining unit is a mandatory subject of collective bargaining.[24] Worker displacement and layoffs, whether caused by AI-powered robots or otherwise, are also mandatory bargaining subjects. The decision to implement new technology or workplace automation powered by AI may also be subject to mandatory bargaining under

---

[22]*First Nat'l Maint. Corp. v. NLRB*, 452 U.S. 666, 682-683 (1981).
[23]*Willamette Tug & Barge Co.*, 300 N.L.R.B. 282 (1990).
[24]*Omaha Typographical Union, No. 190 v. NLRB*, 545 F.2d 1138 (8th Cir. 1976).

certain circumstances.[25] As such, employers also must negotiate with a union before:

- Subjecting employees to discipline for not using new technology.[26]
- Installing technology to detect employee misconduct where employers may use the technology for disciplining employees.[27]

Due to the potential of AI to change the dynamics of work, its use in the workplace could require an employer to engage in effective bargaining. This could, depending on the circumstances, involve discussions on issues like job security, opportunities for retraining, and job displacement caused by the implementation of AI tools.

---

[25] *First Nat'l Maint. Corp. v. NLRB*, 452 U.S. 666, 676-77 (1981); *Fibreboard Paper Prods. Corp.*, 379 U.S. 203, 214-15 (1964).
[26] *King Soopers, Inc.*, 340 N.L.R.B. 628, 629 n. 7 (2003).
[27] *Colgate-Palmolive Co.*, 323 N.L.R.B. 515, 515-16 (1997).

An Important Note

Even if not required to bargain about the subject, parties often negotiate a new technology or automation clause in a collective bargaining agreement (CBA) to remove uncertainty about their respective rights, restrictions, and prohibitions concerning new technology or automation before the employer contemplates or implements either.

If a union does not request bargaining over the effects of a particular decision, an employer has no obligation to initiate bargaining under the NLRA. Mere union protests about a decision, without a formal request to bargain over its effects, do not trigger bargaining obligations.[28]

Employers should also allow meaningful time for a union to bargain about the effects of a change in operations. If they fail to do so, the NLRB could order the employer to bargain over the effects of its decision and award affected employees back pay for a limited period.[29]

---

[28] *NLRB v. Oklahoma Fixture Co.*, 79 F.3d 1030, 1037 (10th Cir. 1996).
[29] *Transmarine Navigation Corp.*, 170 N.L.R.B. 389 (1968).

Nevertheless, although Section 8(d) of the NLRA requires an employer and a union representing its employees to meet and confer in good faith concerning wages, hours, and other terms and conditions of employment, it does *not* require either party to agree to a proposal or make a concession in bargaining.[30] Therefore, if labor and management cannot reach an agreement, an employer may still ultimately implement its decision involving the use of AI, subject to certain procedural requirements (discussed below).

If an agreement cannot be reached by mutual consent, an employer would then have to comply with the impasse procedures under the NLRB. An impasse is a deadlock where parties, after exhaustive good-faith negotiations, each take unwavering bargaining positions, with neither party willing to make further concessions to reach an agreement.[31]

---

[30] 29 U.S.C. § 158(d); see also *Phelps Dodge Specialty Copper Prods. Co.*, 337 N.L.R.B. 455 (2002) and *J & C Towing Co.*, 307 N.L.R.B. 198 (1992).
[31] *Taft Broad. Co.*, 163 N.L.R.B. 475 (1967).

In essence, if the parties have reached an impasse for an overall agreement, the employer may unilaterally implement its final offer, changing wages, hours, and working conditions.[32] However, the employer may not make changes that it had not proposed during bargaining before impasse. Although the employer may choose to implement all of its proposals upon reaching an impasse, it has no obligation to do so. Rather, the employer may select which proposals to implement once it reaches the point of impasse, unless it has consistently presented its entire proposal as a complete package, in which case it must implement the whole package or nothing at all.[33]

California Public Sector Employers and Labor Relations

For California public sector employers, such as state government, municipalities, public education (K-12 as well as higher education), transit, and special districts, various statutes govern public sector labor

---

[32]*National Labor Relations Board v. Crompton-Highland Mills, Inc.*, 337 U.S. 217 (1949).
[33]*Emhart Industries, Hartford Div. v. NLRB*, 907 F.2d 372 (2d Cir. 1990).

relations.[34] Primarily, the Meyers-Milias-Brown Act (MMBA) governs labor relations for public employers and employees. The MMBA is similar to the NLRA in its interpretation involving the adaptation of new technology, including AI.

The MMBA, establishes that "wages, hours, and other terms and conditions of employment between public employers and public employee organizations" are subject to meet and confer.[35] "Public employee" means any person employed by any public agency, including employees of the fire departments and fire services of counties, cities, cities and counties, districts, and other political subdivisions of the state, excepting

---

[34]Among the various statutes, see the Educational Employment Relations Act (EERA) of 1976, Gov't Code §§ 3540 et seq.; the State Employer-Employee Relations Act of 1978, Gov't Code §§ 3512 et seq.; the Higher Education Employer-Employee Relations Act (HEERA) of 1979, Gov't Code §§ 3560 et seq.; the Meyers-Milias-Brown Act (MMBA) of 1968, Gov't Code §§ 3500 et seq.; the Los Angeles County Metropolitan Transportation Authority Transit Employer-Employee Relations Act of 2003, Pub. Util. Code §§ 99560 et seq.; the Trial Court Interpreter Employment and Labor Relations Act, Gov't Code §§ 71800 et seq.; the Trial Court Employment Protection and Governance Act, Gov't Code §§ 71600 et seq.; and the Judicial Council Employer-Employee Relations Act of 2018, Gov't Code §§ 3524.50–3524.81.
[35]California Government Code, Chapter 10, Local Public Employee Organizations, §§ 3500–3511, Gov't Code § 3500(a).

those persons elected by popular vote or appointed to office by the Governor of this state.[36]

Similar to the NLRA, public employers are not required to bargain about subjects within management's prerogative.[37] However, a subject within the scope of representation if:[38]

- It is logically and reasonably related to hours, wages, or an enumerated term and condition of employment.
- The subject is of such concern to both management and the employees that conflict is likely to occur, and the mediatory influence of collective negotiations is the appropriate means of resolving the conflict.
- The employer's obligation to negotiate would not significantly abridge its freedom to exercise those

---

[36]California Government Code, Chapter 10, Local Public Employee Organizations, §§ 3500–3511, Gov't Code § 3501(d).

[37]*Building Material & Construction Teamsters' Union Local 216 v. Farrell*, 41 Cal. 3d 651, 660, 663, 224 Cal. Rptr. 688 (1986); *Solano County Employees Assn. v. County of Solano*, 136 Cal. App. 3d 256, 263-64, 186 Cal. Rptr. 147 (1982); *San Jose Peace Officers Assn. v. City of San Jose*, 78 Cal. App. 3d 935, 144 Cal. Rptr. 638 (1978), reh'g denied (1978), review denied (1978).

[38]*Healdsburg Union High School District and Healdsburg Union School District/San Mateo City School District*, PERB Decision No. 177E (1981).

managerial prerogatives essential to the achievement of its mission.

Except in cases of emergency, the public agency must give reasonable written notice to each recognized employee organization affected by any ordinance, rule, resolution, or regulation directly relating to matters within the scope of representation proposed to be adopted by the governing body or the designated boards and commissions and shall give the recognized employee organization the opportunity to meet and confer with the agency.[39]

The duty to bargain effects occur when the public employer institutes a change in a fundamental management prerogative that is outside the scope of bargaining, but that change has an impact on wages, hours, or terms and conditions of employment. Specifically, the California Supreme Court has provided a three-part test under the MMBA for determining

[39]California Government Code, Chapter 10, Local Public Employee Organizations, §§ 3500–3511, Gov't Code § 3504.5(a).

whether there is a duty to bargain over the effects on wages, hours, and other terms and conditions:[40]

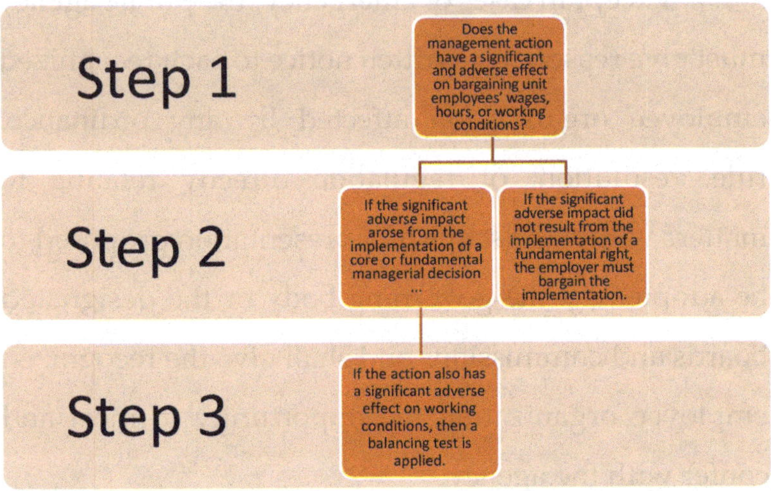

The public employer has a duty to provide reasonable notice and an opportunity to bargain before it implements a decision within its managerial prerogative that has reasonably foreseeable effects (not only actual impacts) on negotiable terms and conditions of employment. An allegation that the employer failed to provide the required notice states a

[40] *Claremont Police Officers Ass'n v. City of Claremont*, 39 Cal. 4th 623, 47 Cal. Rptr. 3d 69 (2006).

prima facie case of failure to bargain in good faith.[41] In order to trigger the duty to bargain over the impact of a non-negotiable management decision, a union must demand to bargain the impacts, not the decision itself.[42] If the union does not demand to bargain the reasonably foreseeable effects after receiving the employer's notice, it waives its right to do so, and this is an affirmative defense that the employer must raise in any unfair practice proceeding.

As such, implementing AI that alters the work of unionized employees will likely trigger impact (effects) bargaining for public employers, and public employers should be prepared to meet with their bargaining units over the impacts of adapting the new technology prior to implementation.

In the event of allegations that a public employer violated the Act, the California Public

---

[41]*County of Santa Clara*, PERB Decision No. 2321-M, 38 PERC 30 (2013); *Rio Hondo Community College Dist.*, PERB Decision No. 2313, 37 PERC 197 (2013).; *California State Univ.*, PERB Decision No. 2287-H, 37 PERC 79 (2012).

[42]*Pasadena Area Community College Dist.*, PERB Decision No. 2218, 36 PERC 80 (2011).

Employment Relations Board (PERB) has exclusive jurisdiction to review and interpret the Act and its applicability to local agencies, including the authority to determine alleged violations of the Act and agency regulations adopted pursuant to the Act, and whether the parties are negotiating in good faith and what matters are subject to the duty to negotiate.

Is AI Now "Contracting Out" Bargaining Unit Work?

The Supreme Court has held that the "contracting out" of work traditionally performed by bargaining unit employees is a mandatory subject of bargaining under the NLRA and termination of employment resulting from contracting out.[43] As such, in cases where AI would replace or eliminate work currently performed by unionized employees and work that is traditionally considered to be "union work," it would trigger bargaining requirements.

In a practical sense, given the rapidly evolving nature of AI and its continued growth and

---

[43] *Fibreboard Paper Products Corp. v. NLRB*, 379 U.S. 203, 210 (1964).

development, it may not be clear from the onset of its adoption whether AI would replace or eliminate bargaining unit work. However, to the extent that it is foreseeable AI may result in the above, employers may wish to assess its bargaining obligations, as well as whether it may be strategically advantageous to begin dialogues with the union early, so that these issues can be addressed early on prior to full adoption.

The Potential Impact of AI on Wages

Although it is possible some companies will raise pay as employees take on new tasks, some experts, including Massachusetts Institute of Technology (MIT) economics professor Daron Acemoglu, are doubtful all workers will see pay rises as AI pushes them to do more varied work.[44] Specifically, in a 2019 research paper with colleague Pascual Restrepo, Acemoglu wrote that we "should not expect automation to create wage increases commensurate with productivity growth." One reason, he believes, is that financial gains realized

---

[44]Daron Acemoglu and Pascual Restrepo, "Automation and New Tasks: How Technology Displaces and Reinstates Labor," *Journal of Economic Perspectives* 33, no. 2 (Spring 2019): 3–30.

from increased productivity are generally absorbed by the company.

Similarly, according to an economic study by the White House Council of Economic Advisors of automation in blue-collar jobs, Germany, France, Spain and The Netherlands saw revenue from productivity gains go to shareholders and not to the salaries of warehouse workers.[45]

For now, it is not clear which types of employees will find their pay most affected by AI. However, as AI evolves, we can certainly expect to see changes to compensation as a result of job functions changing across industries and occupations.

Wage and Hour Issues with AI

Employers reorganizing their workforce to incorporate the use of AI and robots must also consider

[45]Council of Economic Advisers, *The Impact of Artificial Intelligence on the Future of Workforces in the European Union and the United States of America: An Economic Study Prepared in Response to the US-EU Trade and Technology Council Inaugural Joint Statement* (Washington, DC: White House, December 5, 2022).

potential compliance issues under applicable federal and state wage and hour laws.

For example, robotic automation may change the supervisory responsibilities of some employees previously classified as exempt from the minimum wage and overtime requirements of the Fair Labor Standards Act (FLSA).[46] To qualify for the executive exemption (also known as the managerial exemption), an employee must satisfy both the salary test and the duties test. Among other things, the employee must both:

- Customarily and regularly direct the work of two or more other full-time employees or their equivalent.[47]
- Have the authority to hire or fire other employees.[48]

---

[46]29 U.S.C. § 203.
[47]29 C.F.R. §§ 541.100(a)(3), 541.104.
[48]29 C.F.R. §§ 541.100(a)(4), 541.105.

An Important Note

Applicable state laws may impose different standards to be exempt from minimum wage and overtime.

Under the current legal framework, it is unclear whether any employee can qualify for the executive exemption by merely "directing the work" of robots. The definition of employment under the FLSA ("suffer or permit to work") may be broad enough to encompass services performed by robots. However, it is less clear what it means to "hire or fire" a robot. It is likely that further legislative, administrative, or judicial guidance will clarify this issue in the future.

The Hollywood Strike - A Practical Study in Labor Concerns and AI Use

AI has emerged as a key issue in the strikes by screenwriters and actors against television and movie production companies, being called an "existential threat" to creative professionals. The disputes serve as a learning lesson for successfully incorporating AI into your business models with minimal disruption.

In 2023, for the first time in over six decades, two Hollywood labor unions engaged in simultaneous strikes. In May 2023, the Writers Guild of America went on strike against the Alliance of Motion Picture and Television Producers as 11,500 television and film screenwriters stopped working. They were then joined by the SAG-AFTRA union of screen actors and other entertainers, comprising approximately 160,000 professionals.

AI was the focal point, as writers were concerned that Generative AI (GenAI) tools (such as ChatGPT) could replace them. They wanted the studios to agree that such technology can only be used to help with research or facilitating script ideas and ***not*** generate actual content. They also sought to block existing works created by union professionals from being used as source material to train AI to create new original material.

Similarly, actors have expressed similar concerns about AI. Specifically, the actors fear the technology could be used to replicate their likeness and voice without their consent or proper compensation. During the course of these strikes, Union President Fran Drescher shared strong words in opposition to GenAI in Hollywood, saying, "If we do not stand tall right now, we are all going to be in jeopardy of being replaced by machines."

In the end, the WGA came away from a nearly 150-day strike with assurances that AI cannot be used to "undermine" a writer's credit and requirements for Hollywood studios to disclose if any material provided to a writer was produced by AI, while allowing writers to individually use AI tools if they choose. The studios agreed that AI may not write or rewrite original material, and AI-generated material will not be considered source material under the agreement.

A writer can choose to use AI when performing writing services. However, they cannot be required to use AI software when performing writing services. Furthermore, studios must now disclose to the writer if any materials given to the writer have been generated by AI or incorporate AI-generated material. Lastly, the WGA reserves the right to assert writers' material was used to train AI which has been prohibited by the collective bargaining agreement or other law.

For SAG-AFTRA, the agreement requires studios to seek an actor's consent before a "digital replica" of their voice or likeness can be used and to provide compensation for when that facsimile is used, similar to if the performer were on set.

The Hollywood strikes demonstrate a strong distrust of AI and apprehension of utilizing it in the workplace. It was essentially a "do or die" moment for labor in this instance, and they *did*, fighting to ensure that AI did not replace them.

Concerns by Hospitality Workers in Las Vegas

In addition to the Hollywood strikes, labor unions in Las Vegas have sought assurances that AI will not lead to widespread job losses and the erosion of human-centered services. In this case, the major focus is on the customer service and hospitality sectors in one of the world's most celebrated cities, which welcomes millions of visitors each year. Nonetheless, AI is front and center here as well, acting as the driver behind the desired contracts labor sought. It is likely that this trend will continue across industries, with labor wanting assurances upfront. Equally important, employers should carefully consider how to approach the implementation of AI with a unionized workforce, whether through policy, ethics, or practical implementation.

Practical Tips for Implementing AI in a Represented (Unionized) Workforce

With the adaptation of AI in the workplace, here are some issues that unions will likely wish to address with employers. As you consider how AI might impact and benefit your operations, the following tactics may be helpful:

Utilize Extra Manpower

Strategically reallocate human resources freed up by AI automation to areas that require real human expertise and creativity. Doing so will boost operations and morale. Explore opportunities for employees to take on higher-value tasks, contribute to innovation initiatives, or engage in customer-centric activities that enhance overall business performance.

Provide Job Security Commitments

Giving assurances regarding job security and stability amidst AI implementation is important. Clearly communicate organizational policies and commitments regarding workforce retention to prevent people from assuming the worst. While jobs may change drastically in the years to come, employers' assurances that individual employees are not going away will go a long way with the workforce.

Invest in Training and Upskilling

Investing in training and upskilling programs to empower employees with the skills and knowledge needed to adapt to the changing technological landscape will not just benefit your businesses operationally, but it will clearly show employees that they are not just being tossed to the wayside for "the robots." Actions speak louder than words, and that certainly applies here.

Alleviate Fear

Acknowledging the concerns and uncertainties surrounding AI adoption among the workforce will help establish a sense of trust. Consider proactively engaging employees in discussions about the purpose and implications of AI technologies, addressing misconceptions head-on, acknowledging any "unknowns," and highlighting the potential benefits they offer.

Collaborate With HR And Legal Partners

Partner closely with HR professionals and legal advisors to navigate labor and ethical issues and regulatory considerations associated with AI implementation. Developing comprehensive strategies that address workforce concerns while ensuring compliance with relevant laws, ethical standards and regulations will strengthen your organization.

Communication is Not Just About Words

At the end of the day, this boils down to one central concept: Historically, labor has valued one thing perhaps more than any other—communication. Bearing this in mind, it is vital to map out at what stage to communicate with labor regarding the shift to a more AI-centered workplace. Many employers have what are called labor-management committees. These committees serve as forums where both parties can discuss emerging technologies, including AI, and their potential impact on the workforce, talking through things that impact both labor and management.

Why is this so important? Because AI is a technology that moves very quickly. Within just a couple of months, some operations that might have been in a much more infant stage are now ready for implementation. Remember, AI is not living "one life at a time," so to speak—it takes advantage of all users that feed data into its algorithm simultaneously.

Strategic planning and getting buy-in from labor can help foster two important qualities: trust and cooperation, ensuring that AI integration enhances productivity and efficiency while safeguarding the rights and livelihoods of workers. Truly strategic employers will recognize the importance of addressing fears and uncertainties among their workforce by implementing transparent communication channels, providing comprehensive training programs, and making commitments to job security.

A Closing Thought: Human Fears About AI Show the Truth About Human Nature

One thing I have learned over my time working in HR and practicing law is this: when people do not know what is going on, they jump to assume the worst-case scenario. Why do we do this? Because it is the default for most people. For example, say I had a medical exam this morning but have not heard from the doctor by the end of the day. If you are like me, you will begin thinking how something terrible is wrong with you come 4:30 PM. Most likely, the reality is that the doctor is just busy and has not gotten around to contacting you yet, but it still causes you to wonder endlessly.

Being able to communicate clearly and honestly (not just verbally, but in action) often helps employees along in the process. Even more, those who truly care about what they do may take this opportunity to learn new skills and deliver even more value to the company. At the end of the day, employers are looking not just for the quantity of employees, but also the quality of employees—and helping quality employees prepare through clear communication is key to bringing your organization to the next level.

Chapter Five

Potential Legal Issues with AI in the Employment Setting

There is so much unknown about the future of the law and its intersection with the emerging world of AI technology. I have often thought, "When I publish this book, I might need to write a new edition every year because of how quickly things will change due to the nature of the technology." The reality today is that you simply cannot ignore the ways in which a landmark case could impact the legal field in the years to come. This is a critical consideration to keep in mind when building your business with AI.

So far, I have discussed the "unknowns" and the rapid nature in which this technology will likely progress, but we have not spent much time discussing the legal considerations associated with the emergence of these tools. This is where that conversation will take place, as the infusion of AI into the workplace introduces several legal considerations that both employers and employees alike will need to think through.

With this in mind, here are some key questions to consider in the context of AI and the workforce:

- Could AI increase the risk of discrimination and bias?
- What is the impact of transparency in employee communications?
- How does AI interact with data protection and privacy?
- What about job displacement and skills development?
- Will AI impact how we define and engage employees?
- How can we demonstrate the ethical use of AI?

AI Discrimination

One particularly significant risk factor is vulnerability to discrimination claims stemming from the use of AI and its unintended outcomes. Employers are already utilizing forms of AI to assist in the hiring and recruitment process, posing legal implications in the labor and employment space. The Equal Employment Opportunity Commission (EEOC) has weighed in on this issue several times.

While there is currently no federal law or regulations that specifically regulate AI in the workplace, in May 2022, the EEOC published guidance aimed to help U.S. employers navigate compliance with the Americans with Disabilities Act (ADA) while using AI in the workplace. The same day, the Department of Justice posted its own guidance regarding AI-related disability discrimination. Both sets of guidance outline potential ways AI and automated hiring tools could violate the ADA.

Anti-discrimination laws generally prohibit discrimination against individuals in the terms or conditions of employment based on their membership in one or more protected classes.

Federally protected classes include:[49]

- Race
- Color
- Religion or creed
- National origin or ancestry
- Sex (including gender, pregnancy, sexual orientation, and gender identity)
- Age
- Physical or mental disability
- Veteran status
- Genetic information
- Citizenship

In October 2021, the EEOC launched the Artificial Intelligence and Algorithmic Fairness Initiative.[50] Its stated goal is to ensure that AI and other emerging tools

---

[49]Civil Rights Act of 1964, Pub. L. No. 88-352, §§ 701-716, 78 Stat. 241, 253-66 (codified as amended at 42 U.S.C. §§ 2000e to 2000e-17).
[50]U.S. Equal Employment Opportunity Commission. *Artificial Intelligence and Algorithmic Fairness Initiative*. https://www.eeoc.gov/ai.

used in hiring and other employment decisions comply with federal civil rights laws. In the EEOC's view, AI could potentially be used by employers to engage in discrimination or could result in that outcome regardless of intent. The EEOC states: "While AI systems may offer new opportunities for employers, they also have the potential to discriminate."[51]

Through the initiative, the EEOC will examine more closely how existing and developing technologies fundamentally change the ways employment decisions are made. The initiative's goal is to guide employers, employees, job applicants, and vendors to ensure that these technologies are used fairly and consistently with federal equal employment opportunity laws.

EEOC Guidance and Legal Framework

In support of these goals, the EEOC has issued guidance on topics of law relevant to its overall mandate, including:

---

[51] *Id.*

- **May 18, 2023:** Assessing Adverse Impact in Software, Algorithms, and Artificial Intelligence Used in Employment Selection Procedures Under Title VII of the Civil Rights Act of 1964.[52]
- **May 12, 2022:** The Americans with Disabilities Act and the Use of Software, Algorithms, and Artificial Intelligence to Assess Job Applicants and Employees.[53]

This guidance, along with the Joint Statement on Enforcement Efforts Against Discrimination and Bias in Automated Systems issued by the EEOC with the Consumer Financial Protection Bureau, the Justice Department's Civil Rights Division, and the Federal Trade Commission[54], forms the backbone of the EEOC's

---

[52]The Equal Employment Opportunity Commission, *Select Issues: Assessing Adverse Impact in Software, Algorithms, and Artificial Intelligence Used in Employment Selection Procedures Under Title VII of the Civil Rights Act of 1964,* https://www.eeoc.gov/laws/guidance/select-issues-assessing-adverse-impact-software-algorithms-and-artificial.

[53]The Equal Employment Opportunity Commission, *The Americans with Disabilities Act and the Use of Software, Algorithms, and Artificial Intelligence to Assess Job Applicants and Employees,* https://www.eeoc.gov/laws/guidance/americans-disabilities-act-and-use-software-algorithms-and-artificial-intelligence.e.

[54]Rohit Chopra et al., "Joint Statement on Enforcement of Civil Rights, Fair Competition, Consumer Protection, and Equal Opportunity Laws in Automated Systems," *Equal Employment Opportunity Commission,*

position on AI in employment. Employers should pay close attention to this guidance because it establishes the AI use that the EEOC and courts will scrutinize and attempt to hold employers accountable for where it causes discrimination against protected classes.

The statement further outlined ongoing work on AI issues and listed the categories of potential sources of discrimination in automated systems:

- Data and datasets, including datasets that are unrepresentative or incorporate historical bias.
- Model opacity and access.
- Design and use, including the context for use of automated systems.

The potential issue is that AI programs have been found to exhibit or even learn bias, in some cases, despite safeguards being put in place to minimize this risk.

---

https://www.eeoc.gov/joint-statement-enforcement-civil-rights-fair-competition-consumer-protection-and-equal-0.

Technological Resources to Review for EEOC Compliance

Employers use many different kinds of technology in the hiring and promotional process, so it may be easy to overlook certain tools. Although not an exhaustive list, the EEOC reminds employers of the kinds of technology resources to consider when reviewing compliance in light of this guidance:

- Resume scanners that prioritize certain keywords.
- Monitoring software that rates employees on, for example, keystrokes.
- Virtual assistants or chatbots that reject candidates for employment along predefined parameters.
- Video interviewing technology that evaluates candidates based on facial expressions or speech patterns.
- Testing software that provides a score for "job fit" according to personality, aptitudes, cognitive skills, or perceived "cultural fit" based on games or tests.

Under the EEOC Guidelines, a "selection procedure" is any "measure, combination of measures, or procedure" if it is used as a basis for an employment decision.[55] As a result, the Guidelines would apply to algorithmic decision-making tools when they are used to make or inform decisions about whether to hire, promote, terminate, or take similar actions toward applicants or current employees.

This means employers must assess whether a selection procedure has an adverse impact on a particular protected group by checking whether the use of the procedure causes a selection rate for individuals in the group that is "substantially" less than the selection rate for individuals in another group.[56]

---

[55] 29 C.F.R. § 1607.16(Q).
[56] 29 C.F.R. § 1607.16(B).

Quick Tip

Remember to Check Compliance with Federal and State Laws

When using AI to screen applicants, employers should be mindful that the screening technology complies with existing federal and state laws regarding:

- Background Check Disclosures
- Fair Credit Reporting Act (FCRA) Requirements[57]
- Salary History Bans
- Criminal History Bans (Ban-the-Box Laws)
- Privacy and Data Concerns

---

[57] 15 U.S.C. § 1681b(b)(2)(A).

The Risk of Disparate Impact

AI presents a particular risk of "disparate impact," one kind of discrimination prohibited under Title VII of the Civil Rights Act of 1964 (Title VII). Title VII generally prohibits employment discrimination based on a person's membership in one or more protected classes.

Title VII generally prohibits intentional discrimination, or "disparate treatment" in employment, including employment tests that are "designed, intended or used to discriminate because of race, color, religion, sex or national origin."[58] Title VII also generally prohibits employers from using neutral tests or selection procedures that have the effect of disproportionately excluding persons based on race, color, religion, sex, or national origin if the tests or selection procedures are not "job-related for the position in question and consistent

[58]42 U.S.C. § 2000e-2(h) (discussing professionally developed tests); see also § 2000e-2(a) (generally prohibiting discrimination on the basis of race, color, national origin, sex, or religion by covered employers), (c) (same, with respect to labor organizations), (d) (same, with respect to training programs).

with business necessity."[59] This is called "disparate impact" or "adverse impact" discrimination.

Under a disparate impact theory, a practice or policy seems to be entirely neutral but has a discriminatory effect on one or more protected classes. So, while using AI in the hiring process may seem like a neutral practice, the practical application of AI in hiring could result in discriminatory results if it tends to exclude members of a protected class in greater numbers than would be statistically expected.[60]

The Risk of Inference-Based Discrimination

There is a risk that AI may make inferences based on an applicant's religion, age, sexuality, genetic information or disability status learned from either the internet, social media or the applicant's resume or interview. Though AI may not intentionally screen out or favor certain protected classes, AI's choice could cause a discriminatory impact.

---

[59] 42 U.S.C. § 2000e-2(a)(2), (k).

[60] EEOC, *Select Issues: Assessing Adverse Impact in Software, Algorithms, and Artificial Intelligence*.

If the use of an algorithmic decision-making tool has an adverse impact on individuals of a particular race, color, religion, sex, or national origin or on individuals with a particular combination of such characteristics (e.g., a combination of race and sex), then use of the tool will violate Title VII unless the employer can show that such use is "job-related and consistent with business necessity" pursuant to Title VII.[61]

Within the context of litigation, a plaintiff generally shows disparate impact by a statistical comparison, which the defendant's employer can challenge. Under the EEOC's Uniform Guidelines on Employee Selection Procedures, the EEOC often uses a "four-fifths rule of thumb." This means that a selection rate for any protected class that is less than four-fifths (80%) of the selection rate for the most successful group generally constitutes evidence of discrimination.[62] The plaintiff need not prove that the employer intended to discriminate against any individual or group. Furthermore, the employer's motives are irrelevant,

---

[61] 42 U.S.C. § 2000e-2(k)(1); 29 C.F.R. § 1607.3(A).
[62] 29 C.F.R. § 1607.4(D).

even if the employer's reason for using the AI tool was to eliminate bias or increase diversity.

An employer is also responsible under Title VII for its use of algorithmic decision-making tools, even if the tools are designed or administered by another entity, such as a software vendor.[63] Therefore, employers that are deciding whether to rely on a software vendor to develop or administer an algorithmic decision-making tool may want to ask the vendor, at a minimum, whether steps have been taken to evaluate whether the use of the tool causes a substantially lower selection rate for individuals with a characteristic protected by Title VII. Further, if the vendor is incorrect about its own assessment and the tool does result in either disparate impact discrimination or disparate treatment discrimination, the employer could still be liable.

If an employer is in the process of developing a selection tool and discovers that use of the tool would

---

[63]The Equal Employment Opportunity Commission, "Compliance Manual Section 2: Threshold Issues § 2-III.B.2" (May 12, 2000), https://www.eeoc.gov/laws/guidance/section-2-threshold-issues#2-III-B-2.

have an adverse impact on individuals of a particular sex, race, or other group protected by Title VII, it can take steps to reduce the impact or select a different tool in order to avoid engaging in a practice that violates Title VII. To this end, the EEOC encourages employers to conduct self-analyses on an ongoing basis to determine whether their employment practices have a disproportionately large negative effect on a basis prohibited under Title VII or treat protected groups differently. Generally speaking, if such discriminatory practices are detected, employers can proactively change the practice going forward.[64]

The Risk of Disability Discrimination

The Americans with Disabilities Act (ADA) prohibits employers from discriminating against

---

[64]The Equal Employment Opportunity Commission, *Employment Tests and Selection Procedures* (December 1, 2007), https://www.eeoc.gov/laws/guidance/employment-tests-and-selection-procedures.; The Equal Employment Opportunity Commission, *Section 15: Race and Color Discrimination* (April 19, 2006), https://www.eeoc.gov/laws/guidance/section-15-race-and-color-discrimination. Employers should also be aware of how the disparate impact and disparate treatment portions of Title VII may interact. See *Ricci v. DeStefano*, 557 U.S. 557 (2009).

qualified individuals with a disability in all employment-related decisions, such as hiring, promotion, or job termination. The ADA also requires employers to provide reasonable accommodation to qualified individuals when needed to perform or apply for a job.[65]

Certain AI-powered screening and recruitment tools may have a discriminatory impact on individuals with a disability. For example, AI tools that analyze an individual's speech pattern in a recorded interview may negatively "rate" individuals with a speech impediment or hearing impairment who are otherwise well-qualified to perform the essential job functions.

Similar problems may arise with tools that analyze a candidate's facial expressions. For example, certain facial patterns may correlate with individuals who have genetic diseases or other disabilities, but these patterns are unrelated to the individual's ability to perform essential job functions.

---

[65] 42 U.S.C. §§ 12101–12213.

This means that employers should monitor the processes and results of AI tools to ensure that they are not screening out potential candidates who need an accommodation to perform analytical or other tasks in the hiring process or the essential job functions once hired. For example, a chatbot that screens out individuals with gaps in their employment history may impermissibly exclude those who stopped working because of a disability.

In its May 2022 Technical Guidance on AI decision-making tools and algorithmic disability bias, the EEOC Guidance identifies three primary ways that employers using these tools may violate the ADA. These include an employer's:[66]

- Failure to provide a reasonable accommodation needed for the algorithm to rate the individual accurately.
- Use of a tool that "screens out" a disabled individual (whether intentionally or unintentionally) when

[66]EEOC, "Americans with Disabilities Act and the Use of Software, Algorithms, and Artificial Intelligence."

the individual is otherwise qualified to do the job, with or without a reasonable accommodation.

(For example, this may occur if the disability prevents the individual from meeting minimum selection criteria or performing well on an online assessment.)

- Use of a tool that makes impermissible disability-related inquiries and medical examinations.

Reducing Disability Bias When Using AI Tools

To reduce the likelihood of disability bias when using AI tools, the EEOC ADA Guidance identifies "promising practices" and suggests, among other things, that employers:

- Train staff to recognize and promptly process reasonable accommodation requests. *Accommodations may include:*
  - Allowing an applicant to retake an assessment test in another format.
  - Reassessing an applicant's poor test results.
- Train staff to use alternative means of rating job applicants and employees when the current evaluation process is inaccessible or otherwise

unfairly disadvantages someone who has requested a reasonable accommodation because of a disability.

- Ensure third-party test administrators:
  - Promptly forward all accommodation requests to the employer.
  - Contractually agree to provide reasonable accommodations on the employer's behalf.
- Use tools designed to be accessible to individuals with as many different disabilities as possible and engage in user testing.
- Inform job applicants and employees that reasonable accommodations are available for individuals with disabilities.
- Clearly communicate in an accessible format the process for requesting an accommodation.
- Clearly explain in an accessible format:
  - What traits the algorithm is designed to assess.
  - How the algorithm assesses those traits.
  - What variables or factors may affect the rating.
- Ensure that the tools measure abilities or qualifications for the essential functions of the position directly and not by mere correlation.
- Confirm with the vendor that the tool does not impermissibly seek or elicit information about an

individual's disability or health, except and as allowed regarding reasonable accommodation requests.

The Risk of Bias

Harvard Business School performed a survey and found that 88 percent of HR executives learned that their tools reject qualified candidates.[67] The algorithm rejected many qualified job seekers who may be missing just a few skills from the list of requirements. Another factor was a work gap in candidates' resumes for more than six months. These gaps may represent legitimate life events, like pregnancy, military deployment or illness.

As already discussed, algorithms that function in this so-called "black box" present challenges for both employees and employers working within a legal structure that relies on proving intent or causation in AI-related discrimination claims. The problem is that the "black box" of AI may make it more difficult for

---

[67]Hilke Schellmann, "Finding It Hard to Get a New Job? Robot Recruiters Might Be to Blame," *The Guardian*, May 11, 2022, https://www.theguardian.com/us-news/2022/may/11/artitifical-intelligence-job-applications-screen-robot-recruiters.

employers to articulate a legitimate, nondiscriminatory reason for a decision because they generally do not know (and often cannot know) how or why the AI tool did what it did.

This fact is not merely a theoretical curiosity; it underlies one of the most important values in our legal system: decisions that are not explainable are seen as arbitrary, even more so when a computer is making the decision. We all want to be able to influence a human when that person is about to make a consequential decision. Therefore, AI on its own cannot give the complete picture of the situation, and employers should dive deeper into the reasons behind the data to correctly understand and interpret outcomes.

In addition, hallucinatory behavior appears possible even when the AI is using a closed data set. Again, this behavior is a fundamental problem that has yet to be solved: "No one in the field has yet solved the hallucination problems," (Sundar Pichai, Google

CEO)[68]; "I probably trust the answers that come out of ChatGPT the least of anybody on earth," (Sam Altman, CEO of OpenAI).[69] These candid quotations should provide pause to anyone interested in using AI to make consequential decisions with little human monitoring at every stage of the process.

While AI tools offer significant potential to enhance hiring and other employment-related decisions, they also pose substantial risks of discrimination and bias. Employers must be diligent in monitoring and adjusting these tools to ensure compliance with anti-discrimination laws and to promote fairness and inclusivity in their workforce.

---

[68]Catherine Thorbecke, "AI Tools Make Things Up a Lot, and That's a Huge Problem," *CNN*, August 29, 2023, https://www.cnn.com/2023/08/29/tech/ai-chatbot-hallucinations/index.html.

[69]Matt O'Brien, "Chatbots Sometimes Make Things Up. Is AI's Hallucination Problem Fixable?" *AP News*, updated August 1, 2023, https://apnews.com/article/artificial-intelligence-hallucination-chatbots-chatgpt-falsehoods-ac4672c5b06e6f91050aa46ee731bcf4.

Performing Bias Audits

A bias audit within the realm of machine learning or artificial intelligence tools involves an objective assessment to determine the tool's unequal effects on protected groups, including race, ethnicity, gender, and disability. As AI technology continues to evolve and permeate the workplace, it will become all the more imperative to leverage tools such as bias audits and data analysis to maintain fairness and equity in recruitment and decision-making processes.

For example, in New York, the New York City Council passed legislation, effective January 1, 2023, which is specifically focused on regulating AI associated with HR technology, including employers' use of "automated employment decision tools."[70] Unless the tool has undergone a bias audit, it cannot be used.

---

[70]NYC Department of Consumer and Worker Protection, *Comments Received by the Department of Consumer and Worker Protection on Proposed Rules Related to Automated Employment Decision Tools*, https://www.nyc.gov/assets/dca/downloads/pdf/about/PublicComments-Proposed-Rules-Related-to-Automated-Employment-Decision-Tools.pdf.

Before such a tool is used to screen a candidate or employee for an employment decision, the employer must first notify the individual that the tool will be used, identify the job qualifications and characteristics that the tool will use in its assessment, and make publicly available on its website a summary of the bias audit and the distribution date of the tool. The candidate or employee then has the right to request an alternative selection process or accommodation.

Regardless of where your organization is located, employers across the U.S. can work toward inclusive hiring processes and minimize exposure to litigation by ensuring that any algorithmic tools being utilized in the workplace, including those from a third party, successfully pass a bias audit by an independent auditor.

AI in the Age of DE&I

New research from Charter, a media and services company focused on the future of work, found some gaps in how AI has affected historically marginalized groups.[71] The 2024 research, which included literature review, expert interviews, and a 1,173-person survey, noted a striking difference in opinion among respondents.

Charter's data found that over half of Black respondents were concerned about AI replacing them in their jobs in the next five years, which is 14 percentage points higher than white respondents. Female respondents (35%) are less likely than male respondents (48%) to be using generative AI tools in their jobs currently. Additionally, individuals aged 18 to 44 years old are much more likely than their 55+ year-old colleagues to have used generative AI in their work to date.

As AI becomes more widely used, developing ethical and responsible frameworks is paramount. AI tools should be audited for biases before implementation, and continuous monitoring and audits will be essential to ensure that it is free from biases.

---

[71]Emily Goligoski et al., *Playbook: Using AI in Ways That Enhance Worker Dignity and Inclusion*, Charter, October 12, 2023, https://www.charterworks.com/ai-worker-inclusion/.

Employers also need to ensure that a wide range of stakeholders from different demographics are involved in developing and evaluating AI programs so that this technology can be rolled out with intention.

AI Discrimination Case Studies

The case studies we will explore here highlight significant examples of employer liability arising from the inappropriate use of AI in employment decisions. These cases clearly demonstrate how AI technology, when improperly monitored and maintained, can lead to discriminatory practices:

iTutorGroup

In May 2022, the EEOC filed a lawsuit against iTutorGroup, a group of companies providing English-language tutoring services to students in China. iTutorGroup hires thousands of applicants based in the US to provide remote tutoring services. The EEOC alleges that iTutorGroup violated the ADEA by programming its online recruitment software to automatically reject female applicants aged 55 or older and male applicants aged 60 or older. In August 2023, the parties entered into a consent decree for payment of $356,000 and injunctive relief, reportedly the EEOC's first settlement of AI-related claims.[72]

Workday, Inc.

In February 2023, a job applicant filed a putative class action lawsuit against Workday, Inc., alleging disparate impact in hiring based on age, race, and disabilities resulting from Workday's use of AI systems and screening tools.[73] The plaintiff, Derek Mobley, was an African-American male over 40 years of age who suffered from anxiety and depression. He applied for between 80 and 100 positions with various employers since 2018 and was rejected from each one.

The plaintiff alleges that the potential employers all used Workday's AI systems and screening tools, which unlawfully use algorithm-based decision-making and have the effect of disproportionately screening out members of protected classes and preselecting

---

[72] *EEOC v. iTutorGroup, Inc.,* No. 1:22-cv-02565-PKC-PK (E.D.N.Y. Aug. 9, 2023) (Docket Entry No. 24).

[73] *Mobley v. Workday, Inc.,* No. 4:23-cv-00770 (N.D. Cal. filed Feb. 21, 2023) (Docket Entry No. 1, Class Action Complaint).

candidates who were not members of those classes. Mobley's case is one of the first federal cases alleging disparate impact in hiring based on AI use, and although its outcome is pending, it is likely the first of many claims that will arise in the future alleging employer legal liability with the use of AI.

Defending Against AI-Driven Discrimination Claims

Defending against lawsuits related to AI-driven decisions may be challenging due to the complexity of the algorithms in place and the difficulty in identifying flaws in an AI algorithm that may result in adverse impacts. The *"but for"* legal concept will likely be applicable here, holding employers accountable for introducing AI technologies that lead to discriminatory outcomes. For example, AI could possibly discourage someone from applying for a job because the algorithm has determined that they do not meet the job requirements.

This introduces an important question: *What situations really translate to disparate impact?* Is your AI algorithm picking up on certain traits or qualities, such as family status, that inform key workplace decisions? While the AI has a very logical "thought" of how it got there, is it going to result in those disparate impacts? This could lead to a situation where plaintiffs may be able to argue, "*But for* this technology you have introduced - even if you cannot disprove that it was not discriminatory - it resulted in a particular impact." The defense for employers here may prove to be challenging because AI cannot testify in court like a human resources representative or programmer can — *at least not yet*. Even if the AI can testify in court, an open legal question remains as to whether it will be allowed.

Ultimately, these algorithms are, as I like to put it, "garbage in and garbage out." Much like a plant set in poisonous soil, the effectiveness and fairness of AI systems heavily rely on the data they are trained on and the algorithms used. As such, this will remain a consideration for the foreseeable future until it is improved.

Closing Thoughts on Potential AI Discrimination Issues

The entire employment relationship as we know it today is premised upon *vicarious liability*. This means that an employer is ultimately liable for the acts of their employees, particularly because most employers are corporations or some other kind of legal entity. Infusing AI into the mix adds several layers of complexity, as potential bias concerns that could result in discrimination and harassment claims if the data fed to an algorithm includes bias. Disparate impacts against minority groups or other protected classes, such as disability status, remain a possibility—and regardless of whether AI was involved, the employer is still ultimately liable.

This is a critical area where, although technology offers significant efficiency gains, there is also the risk of providing data to algorithms that could result in impacts on protected groups, posing an important consideration for employers to bear in mind in the years ahead.

With all this in mind, one thing is clear - DE&I and accessibility should be promoted as core tenants of any AI program. Careful reviews of existing AI use and ongoing audits will help curb adverse issues. Furthermore, it is crucial to remember: *inclusivity goes beyond diversity.* True inclusivity ensures that not only are the right people in the room but that they are enfranchised and empowered once they get there. The result? Everyone in your organization can benefit from a range of skills and experiences.

Additional Legal Issues and Liability Concerns

Confidentiality

If employees enter confidential employer information into ChatGPT, it could be revealed to other users depending on the questions they ask, potentially disclosing trade secrets, trademarked or copyrighted material, and other intellectual property, as well as utilizing proprietary information from others, thus creating additional legal risk.

Data Privacy

The National Labor Relations Board recently announced that agency investigators should target workplace surveillance and "algorithmic management" technologies that have a "tendency" to interfere with employees' protected workplace activity. General Counsel Jennifer Abruzzo's GC Memo 23-02, issued on October 31, 2022,[74] represents the latest in a series of memoranda restricting employer workplace rights.

Abruzzo's memo asserts that increased reliance on sophisticated technological tools to monitor employee activities on the heels of the pandemic has the practical effect of chilling union and other protected concerted activities and that AI-driven software could use data obtained from such surveillance to make automated decisions that discourage those activities. This is expected to be a regulatory focus of the NLRB.

---

[74] National Labor Relations Board, *NLRB General Counsel Issues Memo on Unlawful Electronic Surveillance and Automated Management Practices*, Office of Public Affairs, October 31, 2022, https://www.nlrb.gov/news-outreach/news-story/nlrb-general-counsel-issues-memo-on-unlawful-electronic-surveillance-and.

Consent, Permissions, and Copyrights

Before providing AI access to enterprise data, the organization will need to determine what data requires consent to provide and from whom; whether formal permissions are required from individuals who have provided written materials to the organization; and what data might be copyrighted, either formally or merely by virtue of having been written. In December 2023, the New York Times sued Microsoft and OpenAI for illegally "scraping" data from millions of the Times' publications to train AI chatbots to provide a competing source of authoritative news.[75] Prior to filing suit, the Times stated that they had attempted to negotiate license rights with the two companies to no avail.

The U.S. Patent and Copyright Office has confirmed that AI systems cannot be named inventors, but humans can use AI tools in the process of creating patented inventions and must disclose that fact if they

---

[75]Michael M. Grynbaum and Ryan Mac, "The Times Sues OpenAI and Microsoft Over A.I. Use of Copyrighted Work," *The New York Times*, December 27, 2023, https://www.nytimes.com/2023/12/27/business/media/new-york-times-open-ai-microsoft-lawsuit.html.

do. The decision followed a case brought by Stephen Thaler, in which he claimed that an AI developed a novel light beacon device. The patent office denied the patent, finding that only "natural humans" can obtain patents, and a federal court upheld the decision.[76] In a separate case, Thaler applied for a copyright for an AI-generated image, which the office similarly denied.

Facial recognition

Using this type of software is a high-risk activity, as recognized by Google's CEO in 2011, who said the company did not release it at that time because it was "too dangerous in the wrong hands—if it was used by a dictator, for example."[77] Data collected by cameras are collecting data that could be used in such applications, with uncertain consequences for "the right to be left alone," even when traversing public places in which there is little to no expectation of privacy.

---

[76]*Thaler v. Hirshfeld*, 558 F. Supp. 3d 238 (E.D. Va. 2021).

[77]Bobby Allyn, "'Too Dangerous:' Why Even Google Was Afraid to Release This Technology," *NPR*, October 11, 2023, https://www.opb.org/article/2023/10/11/too-dangerous-why-even-google-was-afraid-to-release-this-technology/..

AI-Driven Layoffs

While there are no laws that specifically address worker replacement by AI, employers must be mindful of the notice requirements of the Worker Adjustment and Retraining Notification Act (WARN Act)[78] in the case of mass layoffs. Covered employers generally must give 60 days of notice of any plant closing or mass layoff.

> **An Important Note**
>
> WARN Act notice requirements may be longer and apply to smaller employers under applicable state law.

Employers also must ensure that automating the workplace and any resulting layoffs do not disparately impact any protected class of workers, such as older workers age 40 or older in violation of the Age Discrimination in Employment Act (ADEA)[79], as amended by the Older Workers Benefit Protection Act

---

[78]29 U.S.C. §§ 2101–2109.

[79]The Age Discrimination in Employment Act of 1967, 29 U.S.C. §§ 621–634.

(OWBPA).[80] Employers should offer older workers the same retraining opportunities as millennials and younger workers.

Robots and Workplace Safety Issues

Most employers have a duty to provide a safe working environment under the federal Occupational Safety and Health Act (OSH Act) and applicable state laws.[81] The Occupational Safety and Health Administration (OSHA), which administers the OSH Act, has issued regulations governing machines and machinery in the workplace, but there are no regulations specifically governing AI-powered "intelligent" or "smart" robots that work alongside employees. That being said, OSHA has issued some regulations about the features of robots and robotics systems that present unusual hazards and the most common safety systems used to alleviate these hazards.[82]

---

[80] 29 U.S.C. §§ 621–634.

[81] 29 U.S.C. §§ 651–678.

[82] See: Occupational Safety and Health Administration, *OSHA Technical Manual*, Section IV, Chapter 4, "Industrial Robots and Robot System Safety," OSHA Instruction TED 01-00-015, https://www.osha.gov/otm; Occupational Safety and Health Administration, *Robotics: Standards,*

The OSH Act's general duty clause imposes a general requirement on an employer to keep its workplace free of any recognized hazards that are likely to cause death or serious physical harm to its employees.[83] This clause is a catchall provision that can be cited when there is no specific OSHA safety standard applicable to the alleged hazard.

An employer violates the general duty clause if:[84]

- An activity or condition in the workplace presents a hazard to an employee.
- The employer or its industry recognizes that the hazard exists.
- The hazard causes or is likely to cause death or serious physical harm.
- There is a feasible and effective way to eliminate or materially reduce the hazard.

---

https://www.osha.gov/robotics; Occupational Safety and Health Administration, *Robotics: Hazard Evaluation and Solutions*, https://www.osha.gov/robotics/hazards; Occupational Safety and Health Administration, *OSHA Alliance Provides Important Workplace Safety Updates for Technical Guide Assessing Robot Systems*, OSHA Trade Release, January 26, 2022, https://www.osha.gov/news/newsreleases/trade/01262022.

[83] 29 U.S.C. § 654(a)(1).

[84] *BHC Nw. Psych. Hosp., LLC v. Sec'y of Lab.*, 951 F.3d 558, 563 (D.C. Cir. 2020).

Understandably, workplace accidents involving AI-powered robots in 2024 present unique challenges for employers. As an AI-powered robot learns and adapts new behaviors over time, often without the employer's knowledge of the resulting conduct or how the robot "decided" to do what it did, it is unclear whether OSHA may view harm caused to an employee by an AI-powered robot to be within the scope of the general duty clause.

According to OSHA's Technical Manual (OTM) Section IV: Chapter 4, Industrial Robot Systems and Industrial Robot System Safety, in order to protect workers involved in robotic industries, employers should implement a safeguarding strategy using a hierarchy of control:[85]

---

[85]OSHA, *OSHA Technical Manual*, Section IV, Chapter 4, Figure IV-4.

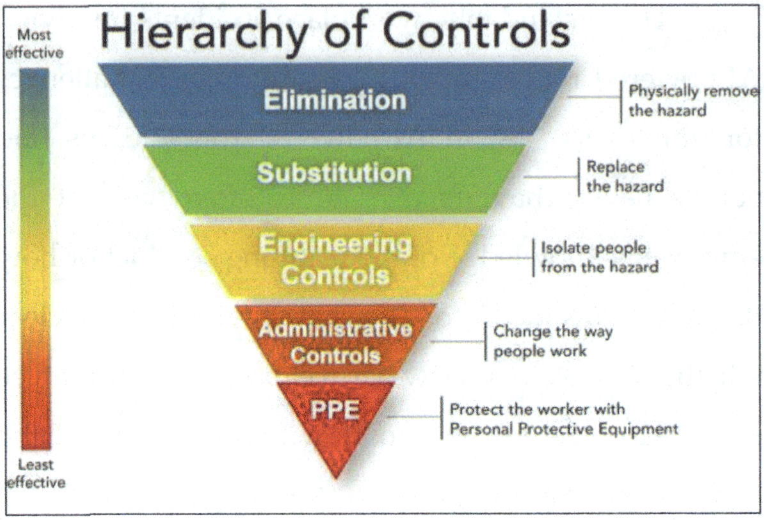

Furthermore, OSHA outlined a 3-Step process, with the safeguarding requirements placed primarily on the machine manufacturer and the robot application integrator, and finally on the employer:[86]

1	Inherently Safe Design Measures	Elimination
		Substitution
		Limit interaction
2	Safeguarding and Complementary Protective Measures	Safeguards & if applicable, Safety-Related Parts of the Control System (SRP/CS) *e.g. safety functions*
		Complementary Protective Measures • *Emergency stop devices and functions* • *Platforms and guard railing (fall prevention) & safe access – building codes & standards can apply* • *Measures for escape & rescue of people, isolation & energy dissipation, handling heavy parts*
3	Information for Use	Warnings & Awareness Means
		Administrative Controls
		Personal Protective Equipment

86OSHA, *OSHA Technical Manual*, Section IV, Chapter 4, Figure IV-5.

Employers may document the risks associated with each task and hazard using the Example Task and Associated Hazard Sheets in Exhibits A and B.[87]

Following a workplace accident or fatality, an investigating agency, such as OSHA, typically requires the employer to take some corrective action. However, employers generally cannot explain why an AI-powered robot did what it did (the black box problem) and, therefore, may be unable to assure OSHA or other regulatory agencies that they have taken sufficient steps to prevent a recurrence of the incident.

Similarly, OSHA can cite an employer for a willful violation if it believes that an employer intentionally violated or shows plain indifference to a regulatory standard's requirements. As it stands today, however, it is unclear how OSHA will view willfulness if the employer cannot understand or explain the reasons for a robot's actions or malfunctioning, especially if the robot has not been involved in any similar incidents in the past.

---

[87]See Exhibits A & B at the end of this chapter.

Robots and Workers' Compensation Claims

In most states, workers' compensation benefits are typically an employee's exclusive remedy for a workplace illness, injury, or death. Employees generally cannot bring negligence claims against their employers unless the employer acted intentionally.

However, most workers' compensation laws do not preclude claims against third-party tortfeasors, leaving open the possibility of claims against robotics manufacturers and suppliers for workplace injuries. For example, employees injured by robots may have more avenues for seeking compensation for their injuries than if the same injury had been inflicted by a human coworker. For a robot-caused injury, the employee can seek recovery from both the employer and the robotics manufacturers.

Use by Bad Actors

Unfortunately, there are many instances of bad actors abusing technology. AI deepfake technology could be used to create fake AI-generated images of people engaging in threatening or hate speech. AI is now sufficiently sophisticated and can create "deepfake" audio and video recordings of people saying and doing things that they did not say or do.

One of the most striking recent examples of a sophisticated AI deepfake scam occurred at a multinational company in Hong Kong.[88] One of the company's finance employees received an urgent email from the company's CFO in the United Kingdom that the company needed to transfer $25 million to another account to allegedly complete the confidential purchase of another company. The employee was understandably suspicious, but his concerns were allayed after he participated in a video meeting with the CFO and other company executives, who explained the transaction. The employee transferred the funds as directed, only to later discover that the meeting, its participants, their images (including official-looking office backgrounds), and their voices were entirely fabricated.

---

[88]Heather Chen and Kathleen Magramo, "Finance Worker Pays Out $25 Million After Video Call with Deepfake 'Chief Financial Officer,'" *CNN*, February 4, 2024, https://www.cnn.com/2024/02/04/asia/deepfake-cfo-scam-hong-kong-intl-hnk/index.html.

In today's virtual world, meeting in person is still the best way to avoid being scammed. While we do not know for sure where the bad actors got the data to make the deepfake video, this example illustrates how such data can be used to construct realistic scenarios capable of fooling even careful employees. This example takes email phishing scams to a new level and suggests that organizations should train employees to verify consequential information, direction, and actions in person or over a direct phone call.

A Timeline of Landmark AI Legislation

- **In 2019,** Illinois led the way with one of the country's first AI workplace laws, the Artificial Intelligence Video Interview Act[89], which applies to all employers that use an AI tool to analyze video interviews of applicants for positions based in Illinois.

  The law requires that employers make certain disclosures and obtain consent from applicants if the employers are using artificial intelligence-

[89] *Artificial Intelligence Video Interview Act*, 820 Ill. Comp. Stat. 42/1 (2020), https://www.ilga.gov/legislation/ilcs/ilcs3.asp?ActID=4015&ChapterID=68.

enabled video interview technology during the hiring process. The law further requires that employers that rely solely on AI to make certain interview decisions maintain records of demographic data, including the applicants' race and ethnicity. Employers must submit that data on an annual basis to the state, which must conduct an analysis to determine if there was racial bias in the use of the AI.

- **In 2020,** Maryland followed with a similar law[90] restricting employers' use of facial recognition services during pre-employment interviews until an employer receives consent from the applicant.
- **On October 17, 2022,** President Biden signed the Artificial Intelligence Training for the Acquisition Workforce Act (AI Training Act).[91]

  The AI Training Act requires that the Office of Management and Budget (OMB) develop and implement an AI training program for certain executive agency employees on the capabilities and risks associated with AI.

  The training must cover:

---

[90]*Labor and Employment - Use of Facial Recognition Services - Prohibition*, H.B. 1202, 2020 Leg., 441st Sess. (Md. 2020) (enacted as Chapter 446, under Article II, Section 17(c) of the Maryland Constitution).
[91]Pub. L. No. 117-207 (2022).

- The science underlying AI and how AI works.
- Introductory concepts regarding the technological features of AI systems.
- How AI can benefit the federal government.
- The risks of using AI, including discrimination and privacy risks, and how to mitigate those risks, including efforts to create reliable, safe, and trustworthy AI.
- Future trends in AI.

- **On March 15, 2022,** the California Civil Rights Department (CRD, formerly the California Department of Fair Employment and Housing (DFEH)) issued proposed regulations regarding the use of automated decision-making tools in employment.[92]

  Among other things, the regulations would make it "unlawful for an employer or a covered entity to use qualification standards, employment tests, automated decision systems, or other selection criteria that screen out or tend to screen out an

[92]*Fair Employment & Housing Council*, Draft Modifications to Employment Regulations Regarding Automated-Decision Systems, Attachment B, CALIFORNIA CODE OF REGULATIONS, Title 2, Administration, Div. 4.1, Dept. of Fair Employment & Housing, Chapter 5, Subchapter 2 (proposed Mar. 15, 2022), http://calcivilrights.ca.gov/wp-content/uploads/sites/32/2022/03/AttachB-ModtoEmployRegAutomated-DecisionSystems.pdf.

applicant or employee or a class of applicants or employees on the basis of a characteristic protected by this Act, unless the standards, tests, or other selection criteria, as used by the covered entity, are shown to be job-related for the position in question and are consistent with business necessity."[93]

- **In July 2022,** the California Civil Rights Council proposed further modifications to regulation.[94]
- **In February 2023,** the California Civil Rights Council submitted a second proposal.[95]

The February 2023 proposal primarily seeks to accomplish the following:

---

[93]Cal. Code Regs. tit. 2, § 11009 (proposed).

[94]*Civil Rights Council*, Proposed Modifications to Employment Regulations Regarding Automated-Decision Systems, Attachment G, CALIFORNIA CODE OF REGULATIONS, Title 2, Administration, Div. 4.1, Dept. of Fair Employment & Housing, Chapter 5, Subchapter 2 (proposed July 28, 2022), https://calcivilrights.ca.gov/wp-content/uploads/sites/32/2022/07/Attachment-G-Proposed-Modifications-to-Employment-Regulations-Regarding-Automated-Decision-Systems.pdf.

[95]*Civil Rights Council*, Proposed Modifications to Employment Regulations Regarding Automated-Decision Systems, Attachment C, CALIFORNIA CODE OF REGULATIONS, Title 2, Administration, Div. 4.1, Dept. of Fair Employment & Housing, Chapter 5, Subchapter 2 (proposed Feb. 10, 2023), https://calcivilrights.ca.gov/wp-content/uploads/sites/32/2023/02/Attachment-C-Proposed-Modifications-to-Employment-Regulations-Regarding-Automated-Decision-Systems.pdf.

- Modify The definitions section, adding new definitions for:

  Adverse impact;

  Artificial intelligence;

  Machine learning;

  Proxy.

- Provide More examples of automated decision systems.

- Explain employer defenses.

- Clarify and modify recordkeeping obligations.

- **In April 2023,** the White House Office of Science and Technology Policy (OSTP) released a blueprint for an AI Bill of Rights.[96]

  The document lists five principles, which are:

- Safe and effective systems.
- Algorithmic discrimination protections.
- Data privacy.
- Notice and explanation.
- Human alternatives, consideration, and fallback.

- **On October 30, 2023**, President Biden signed an executive order setting standards for AI safety

---

[96]White House Office of Science and Technology Policy, *Blueprint for an AI Bill of Rights*, October 2022, https://www.whitehouse.gov/ostp/ai-bill-of-rights/.

and security and directing federal agencies to assess risks and implement policies on AI.[97]

The order is wide-ranging and aimed at advancing safe, secure, and trustworthy AI. Specifically, Section 1 of the Executive Order states:

"Artificial intelligence (AI) holds extraordinary potential for both promise and peril. Responsible AI use has the potential to help solve urgent challenges while making our world more prosperous, productive, innovative, and secure. At the same time, irresponsible use could exacerbate societal harms such as fraud, discrimination, bias, and disinformation; displace and disempower workers; stifle competition; and pose risks to national security. Harnessing AI for good and realizing its myriad benefits requires mitigating its substantial risks. This endeavor demands a society-wide effort that includes government, the private sector, academia, and civil society." *Id.*

---

[97]"Executive Order 14110 of October 30, 2023, Safe, Secure, and Trustworthy Development and Use of Artificial Intelligence," *Code of Federal Regulations* (2023): 75191–75226, https://www.federalregister.gov/documents/2023/11/01/2023-24283/safe-secure-and-trustworthy-development-and-use-of-artificial-intelligence.

The guidance directs several federal agencies to develop guidelines and reporting for, among other things:

- Testing guidelines.
- Cybersecurity.
- Attracting and developing specialist AI workers.
- Best practices on mitigating workplace harm and discrimination.
- Government AI use.

The order also aims to support worker welfare, equity, and civil rights by, among other things:

Directing the Secretaries of State and Homeland Security to take steps to streamline visa timelines and processing and consider rulemaking regarding nonimmigrant visa processes and protocols to help attract and retain talent in AI and other emerging technologies in the US economy.

Directing the Secretary of Labor to:

- Submit to the President a report analyzing the abilities of agencies to support workers displaced by the adoption of AI and other technological advancements;
- Develop and publish principles and best practices for employers that could be used to mitigate AI's potential harms to employees' well-being and maximize its potential benefits;

- Publish guidance for federal contractors regarding nondiscrimination in hiring involving AI and other technology-based hiring systems.

The Future of AI Law

It is anticipated that AI will remain a focus of each U.S. administration moving forward, and employers can look forward to additional regulatory guidance from various federal agencies. Similarly, at least sixteen states have introduced bills or resolutions relating to artificial intelligence in the workplace, all at different stages of the legislative process.

As more states and local governments continue to propose and enact legislation governing the use of AI in the workplace, and as federal regulations develop, employers should stay apprised of these developments that may impact the legality of algorithmic tools in the workplace in the future.

Bonus Resources

6 Best Practices for AI Compliance

1. **Carefully negotiate contractual agreements with AI vendors.**

Make sure that the agreements:

- Obligate the vendor to assume and ensure compliance with Title VII and all other applicable laws in the workplace.

- Detail the steps the AI vendor has taken (or will take) to make sure that its product does not engage in discrimination.

- Contain indemnification and hold harmless provisions in favor of the employer, and the vendor must pay any judgment as well as provide a defense.

2. **Verify testing using the four-fifths rule.**

Ask any AI vendor whether their product has been tested using the four-fifths rule.

3. **Conduct periodic testing.**

    - Do not rely solely on the assumption that the AI tool is compliant with Title VII if it is for sale on the market.

    - Employers should conduct their own periodic testing to ensure that the AI tool does not result in bias or other types of discrimination or disparate treatment issues.

    - Periodic testing should be conducted multiple times a year. Go beyond simply calculating the four-fifths rule and use other measures to determine whether a given AI tool is screening out applicants or employees based on age, gender, or any other category protected by Title VII.

4. **Protect confidential information.**

Avoid providing any AI tools (or large language models) with access to the company's confidential, proprietary, and trade secret information.

5. Respond to detected disparate impact.

If disparate impact is detected, immediately inform the vendor and strongly consider discontinuing use of the tool until the impact is eliminated.

Braving the "Unknown" – 9 Issues Ahead with Use of AI

Here, you will find a short list of the top unanswered questions involving the use of AI and robotics in the workplace. These topics will be key for anyone at the forefront of AI adoption to keep in mind when creating systems, procedures, and policies in the years ahead.

1. **Coverage under employment laws.**

Where workers are replaced by AI or robots, do robots "count" as employees under the various federal and employment statutes?

2. **Liability for "intentional" algorithmic discrimination.**

Can an employer be held liable for the misconduct of its algorithms resulting in "wrongful acts" by the use of AI? Will the AI tools be treated as employees for liability purposes?

3. **Wage and hour exemptions.**

Can an employee who formerly supervised employees but now supervises only AI or robots satisfy the duties test for the managerial exemption? Is supervising an AI or robot the same as supervising a human?

4. **AI or robots as potential sexual harassers.**

If AI or robots "learn" bad behavior from employees and engage in harassing conduct, can an employer be vicariously liable for sexual harassment based on the AI or robot's conduct?

5. **Failure to supervise claims where robots injure employees.**

If a robot engages in violent conduct that physically injures an employee, can an employer be liable for negligent supervision of the robot? What if a robot abruptly spins out of control and injures people as it starts ramming its arms into customers? Are employers liable? Are the manufacturers or software developers?

6. **Robots as part of the bargaining unit.**

Must employers consider smart robots as part of a bargaining unit? Do they have an obligation to bargain "terms and conditions of employment" with the robots?

7. **"Worker rights" for robots.**

Do employers have any recourse against employees who cause physical damage to robots? Are robots entitled to any protection against violent acts by employees under existing laws?

8. **Hacking and security concerns.**

What if employees or outside parties "hack" the AI or robots, causing them to malfunction, divulge trade secrets, or hurt others? What recourse do employers have in those instances?

Imagine the potential for an employee to feed confidential information, either inadvertently or intentionally, into AI systems that can be accessed by others. This lack of proper "guardrails" could significantly disrupt business operations and lead to escalated actions of employee retaliation.

9. **Empathy and workplace relationships.**

If AI or robots develop empathy towards its coworkers, how will that affect workplace relationships, and how will HR handle those situations?

Many of these issues will likely result in further legislative and regulatory guidelines in the years to come. However, as AI and robots are already in the workplace, employers should be prepared to resolve these issues with the help of their employment counsel.

Exhibit A

RIA TR R15.306-2016

RISK ASSESSMENT HAZARD LIST

	HAZARD	SEVERITY	EXPOSURE	AVOIDANCE	RISK LEVEL
1					
2					
3					
4					
5					
6					
7					
8					
9					
10					
11					
12					
13					
14					
15					
16					
17					

Exhibit B

RIA TR R15.306-2016

RISK ASSESSMENT TASK LIST

	TASKS	HAZARDS	NOTES
1			
2			
3			
4			
5			
6			
7			
8			
9			
10			
11			
12			
13			
14			
15			
16			
17			

Chapter Six

HR's Role in Maintaining Ethics in the Use of AI

In 2024, there is currently minimal regulation around the use of AI. As such, employers will need to develop their own principles for how and when they will use AI. As the moral compass of every organization, HR's role in this area is particularly important to establish a balance between key business objectives and ethical concerns.

I have said it before, and I will say it again – AI truly is on the cutting edge of technology. With this technology being so new and potentially transformational, it has an air about it. Some think only the highly tech-savvy have any right to be at the table for discussion and implementation, such as your CIO and other C-suite types, but when it comes to implementation, HR must play a very key role.

Communication within the workforce lies at the heart of this issue. The questions raised by employers and employees alike should be considered with great intensity, and HR is at the heart of working them out. This will not change just because AI is introduced. These are policy issues where HR has the experience to help address everything that is on the line, ranging from the end-user to the ethical implementation of AI.

In my professional experience, HR has always been the voice of conscience, the moral compass of an organization that blends everything together - and it is often successful at doing so. Additionally, HR has historically been the compliance manager for every organization, ensuring adherence to regulatory requirements and ethical standards.

Ethics in Use of AI

Although AI tools offer a wide range of new opportunities, their use also brings up ethical concerns. This is largely because an AI system tends to replicate what it has learned. Machine learning algorithms, which form the basis of most advanced AI tools, are trained on specific data. In this context, AI epitomizes the concept of "you are what you eat." Since individuals select the data used to train AI, it is impossible to avoid bias entirely. Therefore, extra steps must be taken to provide oversight and monitoring.

AI's top ethical challenges include:

- Bias from improperly trained algorithms and human bias.
- Misuse due to deep fakes and phishing.
- Legal concerns, including AI libel and copyright issues.
- Job elimination due to AI's growing capabilities.
- Data privacy concerns, particularly in the banking, healthcare and legal fields.

One of HR's primary roles is to establish and maintain a comprehensive AI compliance framework. This framework should include guidelines, policies, and procedures addressing AI's ethical and legal implications. Additionally, HR should educate employees about the ethical use of AI, legal requirements, and potential risks associated with non-compliance. Moreover, HR should ensure employees possess the knowledge and skills to interact with AI technologies effectively.

HR can help ensure transparency and accountability in AI-driven practices. They can lead efforts to monitor and assess the ethical implications of AI algorithms, data collection, and decision-making processes, ensuring no discriminatory or biased practices occur. Even beyond this, HR's role in AI compliance extends past policy development and involves fostering a culture of responsible AI use among employees.

AI will always need human oversight at the end of the day. Looking through recruitment practices with a trained eye and analyzing data will still be necessary - but it does not necessarily have to be a moral issue every time. It may simply indicate that the algorithm might be swaying decisions in certain directions. As such, HR will serve as gatekeepers, constantly comparing what has been the workforce norm with AI outputs to ensure the stability and integrity of the system.

Confidentiality & Compliance Audits

Employers and HR professionals alike must consider the implications that using AI can have on both confidentiality and compliance. To this end, regular audits are a vital tool to provide continual oversight of AI technology and its application throughout the workforce.

Confidentiality

With the growing adoption of AI for storing business information, organizations need to establish robust cybersecurity guidelines to reinforce employee confidence and prevent data breaches. HR professionals play a pivotal role in conducting these AI audits by thoroughly reviewing data protection policies and privacy notices to ensure compliance with relevant regulations. When an AI solution is provided by a third party, HR professionals should closely monitor how data is used and ensure proper safeguards are in place, including contractual provisions covering incidents such as data breaches.

Compliance

As AI technology continues to evolve and permeate the workplace, leveraging tools such as bias audits and data analysis becomes crucial to maintaining fairness and equity in recruitment and decision-making processes. HR professionals should regularly review existing recruiting and workplace tools for potential bias, including those used by third-party contractors. Including indemnification provisions in contracts can also protect organizations in the event of any legal claims related to AI usage.

By taking these steps, HR professionals can help ensure that AI is used responsibly and ethically within the organization, safeguarding both the company's and employees' interests. The U.S. workforce has successfully blended different cultures, ethnicities, genders, and generations. We should aim to do the same with AI. The key lies in providing leadership, direction, and support to the organization when the time comes.

Bonus Resources

How To Develop an AI Policy

Your organization's AI policy should cover the following basic issues:

- **Guidelines for Using AI.**

Ensure that employees use AI only for authorized purposes, such as drafting emails, letters, memoranda, presentations, and conducting research.

- **Discrimination**

If AI is used in making employment decisions, such as recruitment, performance evaluation, or promotion, ensure that AI systems are designed and monitored to prevent unlawful discrimination

- **Privacy and Data Protection.**

Establish safeguards to protect employee privacy and ensure transparency regarding the collection and use of personal data.

- **Employee Monitoring.**

Be aware of laws and regulations regarding employee monitoring, including consent requirements and notice obligations.

- **Job Displacement and Retraining.**

Establish a framework for handling workforce reductions, including obligations to provide notice, severance pay, and support for retraining or redeployment of affected employees.

- **Fairness and Transparency.**

Ensure that AI systems are explainable and provide justifiable results so that employees understand the basis for decisions affecting their employment.

- **Intellectual Property**

Establish and clarify ownership and usage rights over AI-generated works.

- **Uphold Company Confidentiality.**

Ensure that the organization's most important data, such as trade secrets, private information, personally identifiable information (PII) of employees and other third parties, confidential data, and sensitive matters, are kept secure from AI systems.

- **Ethical Considerations.**

Consider the ethical implications of using AI in the workplace, such as accountability for AI-driven decisions, the impact on job quality, and the potential for algorithmic bias. Establish policies to address these issues.

- **AI Tool Audits.**

Designate an individual (such as the Chief Human Resources Officer) to implement an audit system to carefully monitor and document all AI use.

- **Training.**

Provide training opportunities and resources to help employees understand their obligations under the policy.

In addition, a strong AI policy will comply with any existing and relevant policies, internal controls, and guidelines of the organization, such as:

- Code of Ethics and Business Conduct
- Anti-Harassment/Anti-Discrimination Policy
- Information Security Policy
- Confidential Information Policy
- Privacy by Design Policy
- HIPAA Notice of Privacy Practices and related HIPAA Compliance Policies and Procedures
- External Privacy Notices and Personal Information Processing Policies and Agreements
- Competitive Intelligence Policy
- Copyright Protection and Use Policy
- Corporate Patent Policy
- IT Resources and Communications Systems Policy

Chapter Seven

Practical Steps in Implementing AI in the Workplace

Introducing AI into your organization is a transformative step that requires planning, training, and collaboration. To ensure success, follow these best practices when implementing AI in your workplace strategy.

First, start with a clear understanding of the problem you want to solve or the goal you want to achieve with AI. This will guide your selection and implementation process.

Next, involve stakeholders from various departments during the planning and decision-making stages. This ensures that everyone's needs are considered and increases buy-in across the organization.

Select an AI solution that aligns with your organization's culture and values. Once you have selected an AI tool, pilot it in a small-scale project before a broader rollout. This allows you to identify and resolve any issues before they become major problems.

Establish clear communication channels to ensure that employees understand how the AI technology works and its limitations. Clear communication helps employees use AI effectively and without fear or misunderstanding.

During each step of the AI implementation process, problems will arise. Establish a steering committee representing different functional areas and vested in the outcome to address and resolve issues as they occur.

Strategy With 改善

You probably cannot read this, but you may have heard it before. The Japanese word here translates as *kaizen*. In English, it roughly translates as *improvement*, but it carries a particular nuance that denotes a business philosophy of *continuous improvement* through small, regular changes.

Rather than pursuing short-term gains in your approach to AI adoption, strategic planning should prioritize investments in technologies that offer lasting value and contribute to organizational resilience. This requires a deep understanding of the specific needs and challenges of the organization and selecting AI technologies that address those needs effectively, minimizing the risk of introducing unnecessary complexity or disruption to business operations.

Implementing AI incrementally, phasing it in over time, and focusing on the small wins along the way is a clear and stable path to making this a success for as much of the workforce as possible. Furthermore, starting with a clear end goal and working backward can help ensure success. This approach involves developing policies to facilitate necessary changes for positive implementation, establishing a pilot period to test AI tools, providing sufficient training for employees, and considering the future legal implications that will impact your organization in the years to come.

AI - as it is ultimately just a tool - requires constant re-evaluation of how you are using it. If you have already started implementing AI, a review of what you have done so far and where you want to go is key. After doing so, strategic decisions regarding communication with employees, communication with labor, and policy developments will proceed much smoother.

With this in mind, you will be in a much better position to realize a forward-thinking approach and upskill key employees. Consider what we have already seen – when clerical typing jobs disappeared, related administrative functions did not. Instead, the person holding the clerical job took on more high-level responsibilities. If you are to implement different levels of AI throughout your organization, what will the new iterations of job functions look like?

Preparing for the Future of Work

AI is changing how humans work, socialize, create, and experience the world. Despite the natural disposition many have towards AI, namely the fear of mass job displacement, some studies suggest that AI will create more jobs than it replaces. According to predictions by the World Economic Forum, AI may replace as many as 85 million jobs by 2025 but create 97 million more, resulting in a net gain of 12 million jobs.[98]

Overall, AI is here to stay, and it is essential for the workforce to understand how to leverage it. AI tools can be valuable and complement your organization's efforts without replacing human interactions. The future of work is already here, and it will increasingly be AI-driven.

Training And Development

Training and development are key to fostering a growth-oriented workplace - regardless of whether AI is a factor. If AI is being implemented, this becomes

---

[98]Russo, "Recession and Automation Changes Our Future of Work," *World Economic Forum*.

even more critical. Focus on training programs tailored to these massive changes. Develop a vision across your entire enterprise regarding AI's role while keeping some flexibility, given the nature of this rapidly evolving technology. Forecast out two, five, and ten years to get things moving.

Microsoft's 2023 Work Trend Index highlights that 82% of leaders recognize the pressing need to prepare their workforce for the expanding AI landscape.[99] In this evolving environment, upskilling—enhancing existing skills—and reskilling—acquiring entirely new capabilities—are emerging as indispensable strategies.

To prepare for the future landscape, employers should assess existing skills frameworks and determine what knowledge, skills, and abilities will be needed for AI adoption in the organization. For employees who are motivated and want to be prepared to take on jobs of the future, encourage and embrace their desire to

---

[99]"Will AI Fix Work?," *Microsoft Work Trend Index Annual Report*, May 9, 2023, https://www.microsoft.com/en-us/worklab/work-trend-index/will-ai-fix-work.

upskill and support them in those endeavors. Provide practical and hands-on tasks to immerse employees in the use of AI, allowing them to apply their knowledge and gain valuable experience. Promote collaboration on AI projects, sharing knowledge and insights for collective learning. Establish mentoring programs and encourage participation in AI-focused communities, both within and outside the organization, to learn from skilled professionals and accelerate skill development.

By embracing agility, staying updated on evolving competencies, fostering a culture of continuous learning, and providing hands-on experiences, employers can empower their workforce to thrive in the AI-powered era. As IBM stated in a recent report, "AI will not replace people - but people who use AI will replace people who do not."[100]

---

[100]Jill Goldstein et al., "Augmented Work for an Automated, AI-Driven World," *IBM Institute for Business Value*, https://www.ibm.com/thought-leadership/institute-business-value/report/augmented-work.

Do Not Forget the "Human Factor"

If you have been to certain big cities in Asia like Beijing, Singapore, Tokyo, or Seoul, you know exactly what I mean. Some malls and restaurants in these areas have robots or touch-screen menus in place of greeting and wait staff. With the simple scan of a QR code, your name is on the waiting list, and the menu is downloaded to your phone. When it is time to be seated, you receive a text message rather than a person calling you. Some restaurants even have robots escort you to your table, and you can place your order on your phone. This does not even touch on clearing tables and washing dishes, which is sometimes done by robots.

At the end of the day, AI is not going to replace human-to-human experience. How could it? We all saw how isolating it was during the COVID-19 lockdowns. It is hard to imagine people willingly moving entirely in this direction. We have collectively learned that the virtual environment is just not the same. Being able to hug a friend is irreplaceable; a virtual hug is not a hug at all!

I say this to lay the groundwork for an important point: Workforces seriously considering AI technology and planning to introduce it in the coming years need to think through the process of implementation carefully. AI has implications for training, development, employee satisfaction, and more.

AI is currently the latest shiny new object that employers are eager to adopt. The promise of cost savings, productivity gains, and more do not exactly help keep them sober-minded. While these benefits are important, humans are the backbone of any organization and are the ones who will implement and be affected by these changes.

Economically, a company may benefit by needing fewer employees to perform the same tasks, but several studies show this significantly affects morale and performance. The loneliness caused by such changes is not ideal for retaining employees long term. Employers and HR need to find ways to facilitate connections among employees, especially if AI causes significant changes.

The Risks Of Losing The Human Touch

Employees who frequently interact with artificial intelligence systems are more likely to experience loneliness that can lead to insomnia and increased after-work drinking, according to research published by the American Psychological Association.[101]

Other research suggests that working alongside robots creates psychological challenges for employees, including demonstrating anger and even violence toward the machines. In a recent paper published in the Journal of Applied Psychology, Pok Man Tang, an assistant professor of management, found that introducing engineering robots in a manufacturing setting fueled job insecurity fears and antisocial behavior among employees.[102] They experienced more burnout and were more prone to snapping at one another when upset. In

---

[101]Pok Man Tang et al., "No Person Is an Island: Unpacking the Work and After-Work Consequences of Interacting With Artificial Intelligence," *Journal of Applied Psychology* (2023), https://doi.org/10.1037/apl0001103.

[102]K. C. Yam et al., "The Rise of Robots Increases Job Insecurity and Maladaptive Workplace Behaviors: Multimethod Evidence," *Journal of Applied Psychology* 108, no. 5 (2023): 850–870, https://doi.org/10.1037/apl0001045.

some cases, employees were confused by AI and even yelled at the AI software, complaining that "AI is not getting along with me."

Tang responded to these findings by saying this: "Humans are social animals, and isolating work with AI systems may have damaging spillover effects into employees' personal lives."

Meanwhile, a different study published in the Academy of Management Journal demonstrated that attentive employees who had a high attention to detail reacted more negatively to AI implementation than their peers.[103] As a result of AI adoption, these workers were more likely to burn out, and their performance plummeted. Clearly, AI will have the biggest impact on *people.* So, what can you do to support and encourage "the human factor"?

---

[103]Pok Man Tang et al., "When Conscientious Employees Meet Intelligent Machines: An Integrative Approach Inspired by Complementarity Theory and Role Theory," *Academy of Management Journal* 65 (2022): 1019–1054, https://doi.org/10.5465/amj.2020.1516.

As great as the benefits of AI may be, providing some level of human-to-human interaction is vital to maintaining employees' mental health – and this can take shape in many different ways. For starters, you might implement longer turnover times between shifts, say from 15 minutes to an hour or two. This will provide a setting where employees can talk and socialize while still being productive. Although AI may be great for training and development, removing all human interaction in this facet of the organization may be detrimental as well.

Empathetic leaders should ensure a thoughtful, responsible, and accountable approach in selecting, explaining, and implementing AI tools. This will send a strong message to employees that HR is committed to the "people first" principle.

Bonus Resources

5 Practical Steps to Implement AI in the Workplace

Introducing AI into your organization is a transformative step that requires planning, training, and collaboration. To ensure success, follow these best practices when implementing AI in your workplace strategy:

1. **Define the Problem or Goal**

   Start with a clear understanding of the problem you want to solve or the goal you want to achieve with AI. This will guide your selection and implementation process.

2. **Involve Stakeholders**

   Involve stakeholders from various departments during the planning and decision-making stages. This ensures that everyone's needs are considered and increases buy-in across the organization.

3. **Align with Organizational Culture and Values**

   Select an AI solution that aligns with your organization's culture and values. Once selected, pilot the AI tool in a small-scale project before a broader rollout. This allows you to identify and resolve any issues before they become major problems.

4. **Establish Clear Communication Channels**

   Ensure that employees understand how the AI technology works and its limitations. Clear communication can help employees use AI effectively and without fear or misunderstanding.

5. **Form a Steering Committee**

   Establish a steering committee representing different functional areas and vested in the outcome. This committee will address problems that arise during the AI implementation process.

7 Tips for AI Leaders Shaping the Future

HR is taking a more prominent position today because AI is about enhancing workplace performance, and it is the Chief Human Resources Officer (CHRO) who will pioneer how AI will actually unfold within the organization.

Along the way, leaders should consider the following steps to guide their organizations through AI changes:

1. **Critical assessment.**

   Critically assess the suitability and impact of new technologies – not just AI – before adopting them. As you do, consider factors such as compatibility with existing systems, alignment with organizational goals, and potential risks associated with implementation.

2. **Educate on AI.**

   Become a strategic expert in the power of technology and how it is changing workforce dynamics.

3. **Become a futurist.**

Provide thoughtful guidance to build a roadmap for the organization around AI advancement and its impact on the workforce. Become a visionary leader and predict the workforce of the future.

4. **Get the word out.**

Communicate the efficiencies AI is bringing to your organization often and carry out the message on the benefits AI brings to the table.

5. **Connect people to their work and futures.**

Build job descriptions that are interconnected with AI and allow motivated employees to engage and self-serve their learning and career desires.

6. **Provide stability and continuity.**

While innovation is necessary for organizational growth, stability and continuity are equally important. Adopting an "if it is not broken, do not fix it" approach acknowledges the value of maintaining functional systems and processes that effectively support business operations. It is essential to strike a balance between embracing innovation and preserving operational stability.

7. **Commit to risk management.**

Introducing AI includes inherent risks, such as operational disruptions, compliance issues, and biases in algorithmic decision-making. Develop and implement robust risk management strategies to mitigate these potential pitfalls and safeguard against adverse outcomes.

AI will have one of the most influential impacts on how humans work that we have seen, possibly ever. No one is completely clear on where this all goes, yet those who act and move will play a part in bringing impact, accountability, and guidance to the process.

4 Action Steps for Leaders to Encourage a People-First Workplace

1. **Keep technology ethical and legal.**

Establish usage standards through policy and guidance.

2. **Maintain transparency.**

The very nature of AI generation and function means that tools can act as "black boxes," making it difficult to evaluate accurately what the models will produce and what sources, if any, they are referencing. Maintain transparency wherever possible for all stages of AI models and generated outputs.

3. **Provide context.**

Offer information about the context and use of AI, so employees understand the rationale, which can help reduce fear and uncertainty.

4. **Provide authentic empathy, compassion, and connection.**

Understand that employees may be hesitant or fearful of change, and offer genuine empathy, compassion, and connection. A workforce that relies primarily on AI or robots provides meaningful opportunities for employees to connect, socialize, and be "humans." After all, it is the human connection that builds camaraderie and loyalty to the organization.

Closing Thoughts

As I stated in the introduction of this book, my goal in many ways is just to start the conversation, and that is especially true here. I am not pretending to have any answers, let alone *the* answer. I am merely trying to provide a comprehensive framework that will help you assess and consider all of the implications of AI in the workplace. Our workforce, and perhaps society as a whole, needs us to.

The future of AI in the workplace is exciting and full of possibilities. As technology advances, so do the capabilities of AI, making it an increasingly valuable tool for businesses to streamline processes, improve productivity, and enhance customer experiences.

Implementing AI into your workplace strategy can bring numerous benefits and opportunities to your organization. By following the best practices for implementing AI outlined in this book and adopting a thoughtful approach towards integrating AI technology into your workplace strategy, you can stay ahead of the competition while creating a more efficient and sustainable work environment.

Here is to always looking forward – and to kaizen…

References

- Acemoglu, Daron, and Pascual Restrepo. "Automation and New Tasks: How Technology Displaces and Reinstates Labor." *Journal of Economic Perspectives* 33, no. 2 (Spring 2019): 3–30.
- Allyn, Bobby. "'Too Dangerous:' Why Even Google Was Afraid to Release This Technology." NPR, October 11, 2023. https://www.opb.org/article/2023/10/11/too-dangerous-why-even-google-was-afraid-to-release-this-technology/.
- Cam, Arif, Michael Chui, and Bryce Hall. "Global AI Survey: AI Proves Its Worth, but Few Scale Impact." McKinsey & Company, November 22, 2019. https://www.mckinsey.com/featured-insights/artificial-intelligence/global-ai-survey-ai-proves-its-worth-but-few-scale-impact.
- Chopra, Rohit, Kristen Clarke, Charlotte A. Burrows, and Lina M. Khan. "Joint Statement on Enforcement of Civil Rights, Fair Competition, Consumer Protection, and Equal Opportunity Laws in Automated Systems." *Equal Employment Opportunity Commission.* https://www.eeoc.gov/joint-statement-enforcement-civil-rights-fair-competition-consumer-protection-and-equal-0.
- Civil Rights Council. *Proposed Modifications to Employment Regulations Regarding Automated-Decision Systems,* Attachment C. CALIFORNIA CODE OF REGULATIONS, Title 2, Administration, Div. 4.1, Dept. of Fair

Employment & Housing, Chapter 5, Subchapter 2 (proposed February 10, 2023). https://calcivilrights.ca.gov/wp-content/uploads/sites/32/2023/02/Attachment-C-Proposed-Modifications-to-Employment-Regulations-Regarding-Automated-Decision-Systems.pdf.

- Civil Rights Council. *Proposed Modifications to Employment Regulations Regarding Automated-Decision Systems,* Attachment G. CALIFORNIA CODE OF REGULATIONS, Title 2, Administration, Div. 4.1, Dept. of Fair Employment & Housing, Chapter 5, Subchapter 2 (proposed July 28, 2022). https://calcivilrights.ca.gov/wp-content/uploads/sites/32/2022/07/Attachment-G-Proposed-Modifications-to-Employment-Regulations-Regarding-Automated-Decision-Systems.pdf.
- Council of Economic Advisers. *The Impact of Artificial Intelligence on the Future of Workforces in the European Union and the United States of America: An Economic Study Prepared in Response to the US-EU Trade and Technology Council Inaugural Joint Statement.* Washington, DC: White House, December 5, 2022.
- Eloundou, Tyna, Sam Manning, Pamela Mishkin, and Daniel Rock. "GPTs Are GPTs: An Early Look at the Labor Market Impact Potential of Large Language Models." arXiv, first submitted March 17, 2023, last revised August 21, 2023. https://arxiv.org/abs/2303.10130.

- Eightfold AI. *The Future of Work: Intelligent by Design: Eightfold AI's 2022 Talent Survey.* https://eightfold.ai/wp-content/uploads/2022_Talent_Survey.pdf.
- Fair Employment & Housing Council. *Draft Modifications to Employment Regulations Regarding Automated-Decision Systems, Attachment B.* CALIFORNIA CODE OF REGULATIONS, Title 2, Administration, Div. 4.1, Dept. of Fair Employment & Housing, Chapter 5, Subchapter 2 (proposed March 15, 2022). http://calcivilrights.ca.gov/wp-content/uploads/sites/32/2022/03/AttachB-ModtoEmployRegAutomated-DecisionSystems.pdf.
- Gates, Bill. "The Age of AI Has Begun." *Gates Notes,* March 21, 2023. https://www.gatesnotes.com/The-Age-of-AI-Has-Begun.
- Goligoski, Emily, Jacob Clemente, Kevin Delaney, and Daniel Lee. *Playbook: Using AI in Ways That Enhance Worker Dignity and Inclusion.* Charter, October 12, 2023. https://www.charterworks.com/ai-worker-inclusion/.
- Goldstein, Jill, Bill Lobig, Cathy Fillare, and Christopher Nowak. "Augmented Work for an Automated, AI-Driven World." *IBM Institute for Business Value.* https://www.ibm.com/thought-leadership/institute-business-value/report/augmented-work.
- Grynbaum, Michael M., and Ryan Mac. "The Times Sues OpenAI and Microsoft Over A.I. Use

of Copyrighted Work." *The New York Times,* December 27, 2023. https://www.nytimes.com/2023/12/27/business/media/new-york-times-open-ai-microsoft-lawsuit.html.

- Kochhar, Rakesh. "Which U.S. Workers Are More Exposed to AI on Their Jobs?" *Pew Research Center,* July 26, 2023. https://www.pewresearch.org/social-trends/2023/07/26/which-u-s-workers-are-more-exposed-to-ai-on-their-jobs/.
- LinkedIn Economic Graph. *Future of Work Report: AI – August 2023.* LinkedIn, August 2023. https://economicgraph.linkedin.com/content/dam/me/economicgraph/en-us/PDF/future-of-work-report-ai-august-2023.pdf.
- Manyika, James, Susan Lund, Michael Chui, Jacques Bughin, Lola Woetzel, Parul Batra, Ryan Ko, and Saurabh Sanghvi. "Jobs Lost, Jobs Gained: What the Future of Work Will Mean for Jobs, Skills, and Wages." *McKinsey Global Institute,* November 28, 2017. https://www.mckinsey.com/featured-insights/future-of-work/jobs-lost-jobs-gained-what-the-future-of-work-will-mean-for-jobs-skills-and-wages.
- Meister, Jeanne. "The Future of Work: The Intersection of Artificial Intelligence and Human Resources." *Forbes,* March 1, 2017. https://www.forbes.com/sites/jeannemeister/2017/03/01/the-future-of-work-the-intersection-of-artificial-intelligence-and-human-resources.

- Microsoft. "Will AI Fix Work?" *Microsoft Work Trend Index Annual Report,* May 9, 2023. https://www.microsoft.com/en-us/worklab/work-trend-index/will-ai-fix-work.
- National Labor Relations Board. *NLRB General Counsel Issues Memo on Unlawful Electronic Surveillance and Automated Management Practices.* Office of Public Affairs, October 31, 2022. https://www.nlrb.gov/news-outreach/news-story/nlrb-general-counsel-issues-memo-on-unlawful-electronic-surveillance-and.
- NYC Department of Consumer and Worker Protection. *Comments Received by the Department of Consumer and Worker Protection on Proposed Rules Related to Automated Employment Decision Tools.* https://www.nyc.gov/assets/dca/downloads/pdf/about/PublicComments-Proposed-Rules-Related-to-Automated-Employment-Decision-Tools.pdf.
- O'Brien, Matt. "Chatbots Sometimes Make Things Up. Is AI's Hallucination Problem Fixable?" *AP News,* updated August 1, 2023. https://apnews.com/article/artificial-intelligence-hallucination-chatbots-chatgpt-falsehoods-ac4672c5b06e6f91050aa46ee731bcf4.
- Occupational Safety and Health Administration. *OSHA Technical Manual, Section IV, Chapter 4, "Industrial Robots and Robot System Safety," OSHA Instruction TED 01-00-015.* https://www.osha.gov/otm.
- Occupational Safety and Health Administration. *Robotics: Standards.* https://www.osha.gov/robotics.

- Occupational Safety and Health Administration. *Robotics: Hazard Evaluation and Solutions.* https://www.osha.gov/robotics/hazards.
- Occupational Safety and Health Administration. *OSHA Alliance Provides Important Workplace Safety Updates for Technical Guide Assessing Robot Systems.* OSHA Trade Release, January 26, 2022. https://www.osha.gov/news/newsreleases/trade/01262022.
- Russo, Amanda. "Recession and Automation Changes Our Future of Work, But There Are Jobs Coming, Report Says." *World Economic Forum,* October 20, 2020. https://www.weforum.org/press/2020/10/recession-and-automation-changes-our-future-of-work-but-there-are-jobs-coming-report-says-52c5162fce/.
- Schellmann, Hilke. "Finding It Hard to Get a New Job? Robot Recruiters Might Be to Blame." *The Guardian,* May 11, 2022. https://amp.theguardian.com/us-news/2022/may/11/artificial-intelligence-job-applications-screen-robot-recruiters.
- Shewale, Rohit. "How Many Companies Use AI (Latest Data)." *DemandSage,* March 13, 2024. https://www.demandsage.com/companies-using-ai/.
- Srinivasan, Hari. "Reimagining Hiring and Learning with the Power of AI." *LinkedIn Talent Blog,* LinkedIn. https://www.linkedin.com/business/talent/blog/talent-acquisition/reimagining-hiring-and-learning-with-power-of-ai.

- Tang, P. M., Joel Koopman, K. M. Mai, David De Cremer, Jack H. Zhang, P. Reynders, C. T. S. Ng, and I-H. Chen. "No Person Is an Island: Unpacking the Work and After-Work Consequences of Interacting With Artificial Intelligence." *Journal of Applied Psychology* (2023). https://doi.org/10.1037/apl0001103.
- Tang, Pok Man, Joel Koopman, Shawn T. McClean, Jack H. Zhang, Chi Hon Li, David De Cremer, Yizhen Lu, and Chin Tung Stewart Ng. "When Conscientious Employees Meet Intelligent Machines: An Integrative Approach Inspired by Complementarity Theory and Role Theory." *Academy of Management Journal* 65 (2022): 1019–1054. https://doi.org/10.5465/amj.2020.1516.
- The Economist. "Our Early-Adopters Index Examines How Corporate America Is Deploying AI." *The Economist,* July 1, 2023. https://www.economist.com/business/2023/06/25/our-early-adopters-index-examines-how-corporate-america-is-deploying-ai.
- The Equal Employment Opportunity Commission. *Artificial Intelligence and Algorithmic Fairness Initiative*. https://www.eeoc.gov/ai.
- The Equal Employment Opportunity Commission."Compliance Manual Section 2: Threshold Issues § 2-III.B.2" (May 12, 2000). https://www.eeoc.gov/laws/guidance/section-2-threshold-issues#2-III-B-2.
- The Equal Employment Opportunity Commission. *Employment Tests and Selection Procedures* (December 1, 2007).

https://www.eeoc.gov/laws/guidance/employment-tests-and-selection-procedures.

- The Equal Employment Opportunity Commission. *Section 15: Race and Color Discrimination* (April 19, 2006). https://www.eeoc.gov/laws/guidance/section-15-race-and-color-discrimination.
- The Equal Employment Opportunity Commission. *Select Issues: Assessing Adverse Impact in Software, Algorithms, and Artificial Intelligence Used in Employment Selection Procedures Under Title VII of the Civil Rights Act of 1964.* https://www.eeoc.gov/laws/guidance/select-issues-assessing-adverse-impact-software-algorithms-and-artificial.
- Thorbecke, Catherine. "AI Tools Make Things Up a Lot, and That's a Huge Problem." *CNN*, August 29, 2023. https://www.cnn.com/2023/08/29/tech/ai-chatbot-hallucinations/index.html.
- White House Office of Science and Technology Policy. *Blueprint for an AI Bill of Rights*. October 2022. https://www.whitehouse.gov/ostp/ai-bill-of-rights/.
- Yam, K. C., P. M. Tang, J. C. Jackson, R. Su, and K. Gray. "The Rise of Robots Increases Job Insecurity and Maladaptive Workplace Behaviors: Multimethod Evidence." *Journal of Applied Psychology* 108, no. 5 (2023): 850–870. https://doi.org/10.1037/apl0001045.

Made in United States
North Haven, CT
10 November 2026

22091338R00114